REGIONAL DEVOLUTION AND SOCIAL POLICY

REGIONAL DEVOLUTION AND SOCIAL POLICY

Edited by

EDWARD CRAVEN

Fellow,
Centre for Studies in Social Policy

Softcover reprint of the hardcover 1st edition 1975

First published 1975 by
THE MACMILLAN PRESS LTD
London and Basingstoke
Associated companies in New York
Dublin Melbourne Johannesburg and Madras

ISBN 978-1-349-02735-4
ISBN 978-1-349-02733-0 (eBook)
DOI 10.1007/978-1-349-02733-0

Typeset in Great Britain by
PREFACE LTD
Salisbury, Wilts

Contents

The Centre for Studies in Social Policy is an independent non-partisan organisation for promoting the analysis and discussion of public policy in its social dimension. Its Fellows operate in close touch with colleagues in government departments and universities, and their work is disseminated through journal articles, occasional papers, books, and discussion meetings held at the Centre's premises in Doughty Street, London. The Centre's funds come from a basic grant made by the Joseph Rowntree Memorial Trustees, supplemented by finance for specific studies commissioned by government and other organisations.

Preface

Most nations can hopefully survive, and sometimes thrive, through a great deal of structural political change. But it has to be change which seems worth the risks. By 1974 the United Kingdom found itself in a position in which three questions involving risky change on a major scale were under sharp debate at the same time. They are still under debate today. All of them are of a fundamental kind, because they are about the extent to which there should be formal and binding constitutional restraints on the effective sovereignty of Parliament. How far should decisions of Westminster and Whitehall be subject to veto by members of the European Communities in Brussels? How far and how long should the writ of Parliament still run in Northern Ireland? And to what extent, if at all, should there be devolution of the existing powers of the UK Parliament and Government to Scotland and Wales . . . or to the regions of England?

This book deals with the last of these three questions. It concentrates, though not exclusively, on the implications of devolution within England, because it is only there that the debate is still relatively open and the outcome is not substantially pre-empted by prior emotional and party political commitments. It is concerned less with general constitutional theory than with the practicalities of public policy, in terms of the effects that devolution of national powers might have on the domestic administration of the United Kingdom.

Thus, the first four chapters look at specific areas of policy and assess how far devolution is both desirable and feasible – environmental planning, the public education service, the provision of health care, and the personal social services. The final two chapters look at the relationship between devolution and the continuing operation of first local, and then national government as a whole. The chapters are based on the content and discussion of papers presented by the authors to a two-day seminar held at the Centre for Studies in Social Policy in September 1974, which was also addressed by Lord Crowther-Hunt, sometime Constitutional Adviser to the Government. The contributors are by no means unanimous in their views, and only one of them, Derek Senior, emerges as a full-blown devolutionist. But what all of them have to say is equally relevant to two issues. What price devolution at all? And, if there *is* to be devolution, what should we be especially careful about?

All the contributors draw, understandably, on the work of the Royal Commission on the Constitution, whose Chairman was Lord Kilbrandon, and which reported in 1973.* Throughout the book, the majority report, Volume I, will be referred to as the Kilbrandon Report, and the minority report, Volume II, as the Memorandum of Dissent. The Royal Commission itself will generally be referred to as the Kilbrandon Commission.

I would like to thank all the contributors for their work in preparing their papers for publication, and also those who attended the seminar. The discussion in which they participated so freely contributed a good deal to the ideas contained in the book. I am grateful to my colleagues at the Centre for their help and advice, and especially to Rosemary Lewin, who bore much of the responsibility for organising the seminar and preparing the manuscript.

February 1975 EDWARD CRAVEN

*Royal Commission on the Constitution 1969–73, vol. I: *Report*, Cmnd. 5460 (HMSO, 1973); and vol. II: *Memorandum of Dissent*, Cmnd. 5460–1 (HMSO, 1973).

Acknowledgements

The editor and publishers wish to thank the following for their permission to reproduce copyright material: Controller of Her Majesty's Stationery Office, for extracts from *Devolution within the United Kingdom: Some Alternatives for Discussion*, 1974, and for a map based on one from *Abstract of Regional Statistics 1974*, No. 10, 1974; Drs J. Noyce, A. H. Snaith and A. J. Trickey, for statistics from 'Regional Variations in Financial Allocations', published in the *Lancet*, 30 March 1974.

Biographical Notes

Edward Craven, BA, Ph.D, is a Fellow at the Centre for Studies in Social Policy, which he joined in 1972. He was a member of the joint team of local and central government officials which produced *The Strategic Plan for the South East* in 1970 and then worked as a research officer in the Department of the Environment, being concerned with the social aspects of local authority development plans. His latest publication, with colleagues at the Centre, is *Social Policy and Public Expenditure, 1975.*

David Eversley, BSc., Ph.D, is a teacher and research worker at the Centre for Environmental Studies. He was Reader in Economic and Social History in the University of Birmingham and Director of the Social Research Unit, University of Sussex. He was Chief Planner (Strategy) at the Greater London Council between 1969 and 1972. He is also Chairman of the Regional Studies Association and the Urban Studies Conference and has written widely on urban and regional affairs. His most recent publications include *London: Urban Patterns and Problems* (with David Donnison) and *The Planner in Society.*

Sir George Godber, GCB, was until 1973 Chief Medical Officer at the Department of Health and Social Security, a post he had held since 1960. He had been Deputy CMO for ten years before that and had been involved after the war in the early planning of the National Health Service. He was a joint author in 1944 of *Survey of Hospitals in the Sheffield Region.* He has written widely in medical journals and has considerable experience in the international health field.

A. R. Isserlis, MA, is a former Whitehall Under-Secretary, now Director of the Centre for Studies in Social Policy. He served in the Home Office, the Cabinet Office, and the Ministries of Health and of Housing and Local Government (for some years on regional planning) and did spells as Principal Private Secretary to the Minister for Science, two Ministers of Housing and Local Government, and the Prime Minister. He is a Governor of the National Institute for Social Work and Chairman of the Standing Conference of Councils for Voluntary Service.

Timothy Raison, MP, is Conservative member for Aylesbury and a part-time Senior Fellow at the Centre for Studies in Social Policy. He was editor of *New Society* 1962–8, entering Parliament in 1970. He was a member of the Plowden Committee on Primary Education and a co-opted member of the ILEA Education Committee, 1967–70. He was Parliamentary Under-Secretary at the Department of Education and Science in the last Conservative government. He is now a member of the Shadow Cabinet, and the senior front-bench spokesman on the environment. He has written a number of political pamphlets and was the editor of *The Founding Fathers of Social Science.*

Derek Senior, BA, Hon. MRTPI, joined the editorial staff of the *Manchester Guardian* in 1937 and is now a free-lance writer on planning and local government affairs. He is a member of the Council and Executive of the Town and Country Planning Association. As a member of the Royal Commission on Local Government in England, he wrote Volume II of its report (Memorandum of Dissent). Other publications include *The Regional City.*

Kenneth Urwin, MA, was formerly on the staff of the University of Nottingham and then London County Council, 1950–65. He was a councillor on Croydon Borough Council, 1958–66. From 1965 he has been first Children's Officer, and then Director of Social Services, London Borough of Camden. He is a contributor to *Social Policy and Administration*, edited by Donnison and Chapman, the Cropwood Papers (Cambridge University Institute of Criminology), and *Maltreated Child*, edited by Carter.

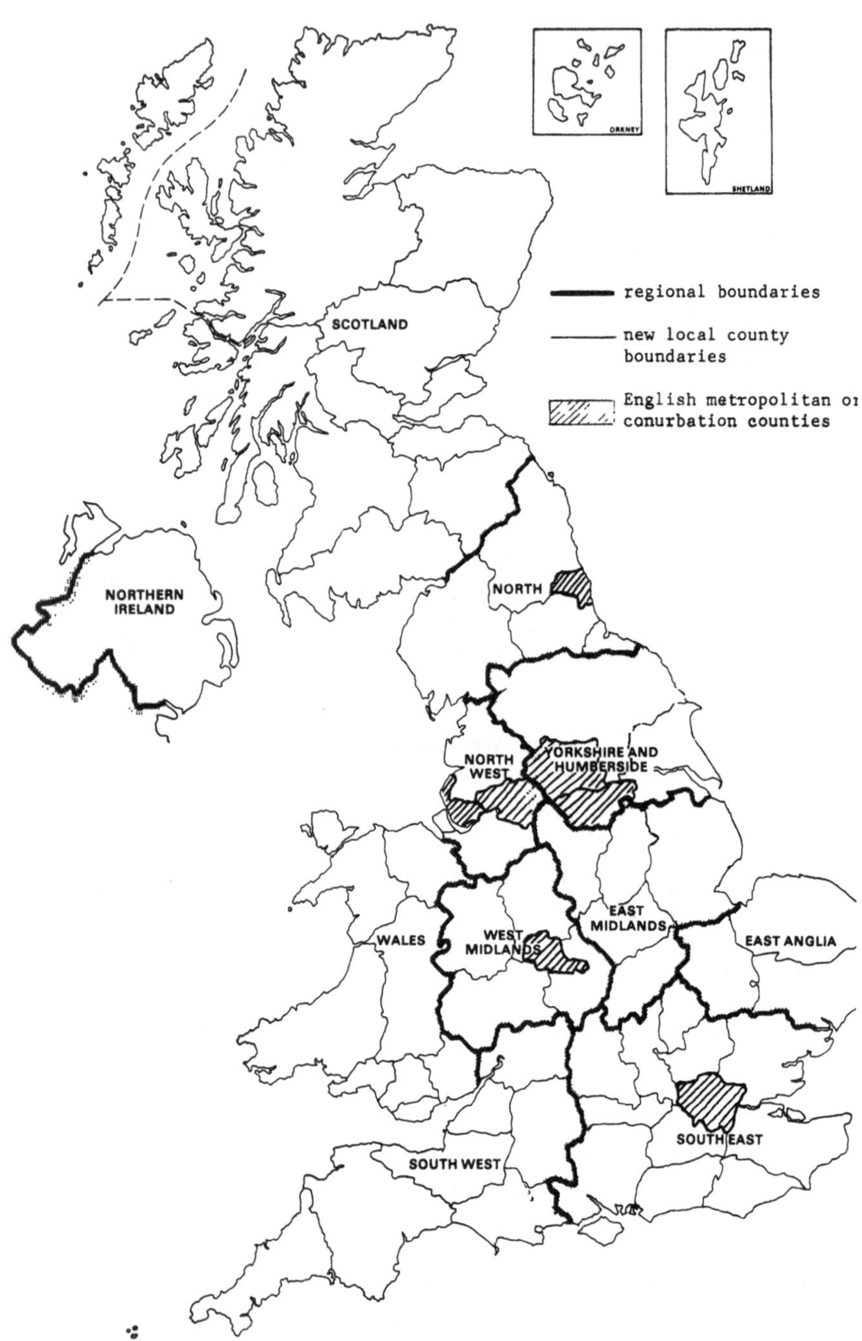

STANDARD REGIONS OF ENGLAND; WALES, SCOTLAND, NORTHERN IRELAND

Introduction

EDWARD CRAVEN

> *... if we can make arrangements under which Ireland, Scotland, Wales and portions of England can deal with questions of local and special interest to themselves ... that, I say, will be the attainment of a great national good.*[1]

This statement was made by W. E. Gladstone during his Midlothian campaign of 1879. In presenting this proposal, he was primarily concerned to pacify a Celtic minority, the Irish, whose political presence both in Ireland and at Westminster was of growing significance. He also wanted to relieve Parliament of an increasing load of business which he believed undermined its effectiveness. Almost a hundred years later, during which time at least a part of Ireland has been dealt with, it is the turn of the Welsh and the Scots, and again it is their political presence and worries about the effectiveness of Parliament which figure prominently in the debate.

This debate is about whether Britain needs a level of government intermediate to central and local government with powers devolved from the centre, and, if so, what form it should take. Historically, the case for intermediate government has been fed by many streams, some political, some economic, some social. They have varied in their strength from time to time and place to place. Sometimes the issue takes the centre of the stage as it did during the Home Rule for Ireland debate in the late nineteenth century; sometimes it remains the prerogative of a few ivory towered academics, and of cranks on the edge of political life. In the 1970s, after the publication of the report of the Royal Commission on the Constitution, it is again respectable to re-examine seriously the case for an intermediate level of government, safe in the knowledge that the political imperatives of

Scottish and Welsh nationalism make the exercise of more than purely academic value.

However, notwithstanding the historical continuities in the argument, conditions have changed since Gladstone's day. The scale of government activity has continued to increase far beyond anything he could conceive or certainly condone. The state has grown enormously in its regulatory powers, and in its role as the provider of social services: its potential for injustice and insensitivity has grown likewise. Moreover, the pace of technological, social and economic change has quickened, creating problems of how government should best be organised to cope with the consequences. The past few years have seen a number of major changes in the organisation of government in response to both fears about its insensitivity and concern with its effectiveness – super-ministries, National Health Service reorganisation, participation procedures in physical planning, local government reorganisation, the creation of new personal social service departments. The Kilbrandon Report, and the firm proposals for separate parliaments for Wales and Scotland, probably completes this wave of organisational reform.

The Commission attempted to analyse some of the broad societal changes mentioned above, and their solution to problems of insensitivity and ineffectiveness was to recommend an array of alternative forms of regional government (which are summarised in the appendix to this book). Their report, together with a large amount of comment and criticism which followed its publication, is substantial enough to provide both a basis and a justification for exploring further some of the questions it raises – and some that it does not.

This book has three main themes. Firstly, Kilbrandon was primarily concerned with Scotland and Wales, and relatively little with England. Harold Wilson set up the Commission in 1968 largely as a response to emerging Scottish nationalism. Even though that movement faded during their deliberations, its re-emergence in the February and October general elections in 1974 meant that the report had to be taken down from the top shelf and thoroughly dusted. Not surprisingly, the only firm proposals arising from the government relate solely to Scotland and Wales, where the nationalist case became effective through clearly expressed political power. England, on the other hand, is regarded as a peripheral issue: not only is there limited regional consciousness, but more importantly, what there is has very little political expression. Yet, as the two dissenters to the majority report recognised, if a case exists for regional government, as they believed, on other than immediate political grounds, then England, the most populous country, should be brought into the reckoning. It is there that the application of the principle of devolution of power from the centre to regional governments could have the greatest effect – for good or ill. Indeed, the very absence of pressing political pressures in England allows us to take perhaps a more sober and objective look at the alleged defects in our governmental system. Focusing on England allows us to consider the problems of the centralisation of political power, uncomplicated by the problems of Celtic nationalism. Moreover, England is different from Wales and Scotland in other respects than the purely political ones. It has had only a limited tradition of regional administration, compared with a relatively developed tradition in Wales and Scotland, embodied in the Scottish and Welsh Offices. Also the reorganisation of local government in England was undertaken on very different principles from those in Scotland. Therefore, the chapters in this book focus their attention on England, although recognising that this may reveal lessons for Scotland and Wales.

Secondly, a major part of the case which Kilbrandon presents can be called 'democratic' in nature. Concern is expressed about the power of the executive at the centre; about the existence of *ad hoc* bureaucracies at regional level which, effectively, are not accountable; about the remoteness of government and the consequent feelings of powerlessness felt by the average citizen. Regional devolution is seen as a way of bringing government closer to the people and making it more accountable to democratically elected assemblies. The Report therefore concentrates on analysing the forms, procedures and processes of democratic government in Britain.

However, regional devolution has other kinds of separate, though related, implications for the man in the street. He is also concerned about the nature and quality of the services which government provides and of the activities it undertakes – employment opportunities, access to decent housing, the quality of the environment, schools for his children, good health care, and so on. While it can be argued that some citizens may gain satisfaction from feeling more in touch with government if devolution takes place, how will devolution affect the substantive nature of government social and economic policy? Will it help or hinder our ability to redistribute resources to those who most need them? Will it enable us to make better decisions about investment in major technological projects? Will it allow our social services to deliver the right services at the right time in the right place? Therefore, as well as being concerned with changes in the forms and procedures of democratic government, we also need to consider the substance of policy which might flow from them. Attempts to answer some of these questions are a second theme of this book. The first four chapters in particular try to answer them by reference to specific areas of social policy. Each writer has practical experience of his chosen area of policy and thus is able to suggest some of the likely implications of regional devolution for the effectiveness with which those concerned can undertake their tasks.

A third feature of the Kilbrandon Report is that it deals relatively little with the implications of regional devolution for the continuing operation of the two other arms of government in Britain, central and local government. The creation of a new level of government would change the functions of these two arms of government fairly radically. Local government is very wary of any more major institutional change; its own reorganisation has caused enough problems. Many local government people believe that, whatever is said to the contrary, a regional government would eventually remove powers from them in a number of fields and make the process of inter-governmental co-ordination much more difficult. At the national level, it is argued that central government would have immense problems in performing its strategic policy role if deprived of executive responsibility in various areas of policy. This issue seemed worthy of closer examination; all the chapters in this book deal with it as it affects specific areas of policy-making, and Derek Senior and A. R. Isserlis look at the general consequences of changing the areal distribution of power in Britain for the future operation of local and national government.

By dealing mainly with these three relatively neglected

themes, the contributors are engaged in a debate which, particularly as it concerns England, will be continuing for a number of years. The rest of this introduction tries to set the scene for the chapters which follow and to highlight the issues which they raise. The next section briefly presents the case for regional devolution because, with the exception of Derek Senior, none of the authors find the case to be very strong. A further section presents counter-arguments and suggests some of the consequences of adopting a scheme of regional devolution. The penultimate section widens the debate and asks whether there are not alternative solutions to the kinds of problems with which devolutionists are concerned. A final section returns to the specific theme of regional government in England, and outlines some practical policy choices.

However, it is necessary first of all to define some of the concepts used in this book, without becoming bogged down in detailed semantic problems. We are concerned with two main processes: first, and most important, decentralisation: i.e. the movement of powers and functions from the centre to territorial sub-national units of government (in this case, the unit concerned is the region, an area roughly intermediate in scale to the county and the nation). There are two types of decentralisation involved: *devolution* which involves either the decentralisation of power to make laws concerning one or more areas of public activity (legislative devolution); or the decentralisation of considerable power to interpret and implement law and policy laid down at the centre, as it applies to the territorial sub-unit concerned (executive devolution). Devolution usually involves the creation of a level of government with comprehensive power and functions, not powers limited to one or two specific areas of policy. The second type of decentralisation is *administrative decentralisation*: this involves the reorganisation of central government responsibility so that personnel and some powers of controlled discretion are located in outposts of the bureaucracy in each region (field administration), but with ultimate authority and accountability resting with the head of that bureaucracy at the centre. Administrative decentralisation does not need to be comprehensive: it can involve merely one area of policy. Final accountability and responsibility for public policy are transferred, usually to elected assemblies, when devolution takes place, but not when administrative decentralisation is involved. The second process we are concerned with is, paradoxically, centralisation: i.e. the movement of powers and functions inwards from the periphery. In England, the system of local government is often seen as being inadequate to discharge all its functions effectively; some of these, it is argued, could be better undertaken if transferred upwards at least as far as a regional level.

THE CASE FOR REGIONAL DEVOLUTION

In essence, the general case for regional devolution was stated by J. S. Mill over a century ago, although in a rather different context: he suggested that society tended 'to impose, by other means than civil penalties, its own ideas and practices as rules of conduct on those who dissent from them; to fetter the development, and, if possible, prevent the formation of any individuality not in harmony with its ways, and compels all characters to fashion themselves upon the model of its own.'[2] Mill was warning of the tyranny, as he saw it, of 'prevailing opinion and feeling', and was asserting that there must be limits to the interference of collective opinion with individual independence. For the devolutionists today, the power of 'collective opinion' has increased enormously; one manifestation of this is the growth of government itself, and another the concentration of political power at the centre. This concentration at the centre is seen as stultifying the individuality of both people and areas, removing from them control over their own affairs and imposing a uniformity which bears little relation to their real needs. The case for devolution therefore is part of a long debate about the role of government and the best way of organising the exercise of collective power. Devolutionists bring to that debate the same basic principles as underline Mill's statement – diversity not uniformity; experimentation not conformity; self-reliance and self-government, rather than external, paternal control. However, while the basis of the case rests on these principles, their emergence in the debate about regional devolution in the 1960s and 1970s takes a specific and more complex form, and it is necessary to deal with these here.

The first set of arguments is about the nature of democracy. The centralisation of power in Westminster and

Whitehall, it is argued, has made it more difficult for the ordinary citizen to involve himself in, and have some control over, the affairs of government. This process of centralisation has also been accompanied by a shift of power at the centre from members of Parliament to the executive – ministers and their civil servants. For most people, especially those in regions removed from London and the South East, government is both remote, inaccessible and more and more unaccountable. The process of centralisation and bureaucratisation is said to have brought our system of government more and more into disrepute; the Attitudes Survey set up by the Commission revealed a high degree of dissatisfaction, and also widespread feelings of powerlessness to affect what government does.[3]

Moreover, some individuals, it is believed, have a wish to participate in running public affairs, an opportunity largely denied to many of them by the remoteness of real power in Westminster. The devolution of power to regional authorities could provide such opportunities: it would release a good deal of social energy and increase active interest and participation in governmental affairs. The region is an appropriate unit for devolution because effective decision-making can take place at that spatial scale, but also for two other reasons. First, there are a number of *ad hoc* governmental institutions already operating at a regional scale – NHS Regional Authorities, water and sewerage authorities, outposts of central government departments, etc. – which, while being nominally accountable to Parliament, are not democratically accountable in any direct way.[4] Elected assemblies at regional level could take over responsibility for their operations. Secondly, it is alleged that some people feel an attachment and loyalty to their region: being a north-easterner or a north-westerner is an important source of identity for many people. Therefore regional government could be underpinned by genuine loyalty and attachment, and could build on the existence of common regional identity.

These arguments relate closely to a general worry about the demise of pluralist politics and the development of corporatism. It is argued that the concentration of political power at the centre has been accompanied also by the concentration of economic and social power in a few large institutions.[5] While there may be some conflicts between these concentrations of power, the most striking trend is towards their co-operation and joint management of a growing proportion of the nation's affairs. This co-operation involves the adjustment of policy by all the institutions concerned, and certainly would involve the adjustment of social policy to achieve a general consensus. Pahl and Winkler have recently analysed the negotiations between TUC, government and CBI in this light and suggest that 'a corporatist system will be introduced in Britain by 1980.'[6] If one accepts this case, the relevance of regional devolution is clear. Devolution from the centre could break up the concentration of political power and create a number of powerful semi-autonomous units of government in the regions, which would reintroduce a significant degree of pluralism into the political system at least. The further development of corporatism in this situation would be much more difficult.

Two points about these democratic arguments are particularly important for our purposes. In the first place, the effects of centralisation of power and the benefits consequential on its break-up apply just as much to the English as to the Welsh and Scots. It is true that the latter have a much stronger basis of common identity on which to build regional government, yet, if the general case is accepted, the English experience feelings of powerlessness just as much as the Celtic minorities. The *ad hoc* regional institutions in England are even more unaccountable than in Scotland and Wales, where a minister, answerable to Parliament, in the form of the respective secretary of state, has responsibility for many of them. Moreover, devolution of power to Scotland and Wales, which together represent only about 15 per cent of the total population of the United Kingdom, can hardly be judged a severe blow at the concentration of political power at the centre. If the argument is about incipient nationalism, then devolution to Scotland and Wales is of much greater significance; but if the argument is about the centralisation of political power and what should be done about it, the primary concern must be with England. This distinction is one which is reflected in the majority and minority reports of the Royal Commission. The majority were probably more concerned with nationalism, which influenced them in rejecting devolution in England; the dissenters, Lord Crowther-Hunt and Professor Alan Peacock, were probably more concerned with the problem of centralisation, which led them to recommend executive devolution to the English regions.

Secondly, the 'democratic' benefits of devolution can accrue, without the substance of public policy changing at all. It is possible to imagine a situation in which regional authorities would pursue policies and provide services very similar to those the centre, under our present system, would have provided. The change in process and procedures therefore might not affect the nature of the product. In this situation, if the devolutionists are right, the people in each region would feel less powerless, would participate more, feel a greater sense of common identity, and be generally less dissatisfied with their government than previously. Thus the benefits could largely be psychological, rather than substantive. This raises the issue of whether these psychological benefits might not be produced by changes slightly less radical and disruptive than regional devolution. We will return to this later.

However, most devolutionists would argue that devolution should and would have an effect on the nature of public policy. This introduces a second set of arguments which revolve around the need for diversity. It is argued that the concentration of power at the centre does not do justice to the diversity of social and economic conditions in different parts of Britain. Civil servants and ministers in Whitehall, it is said, cannot know what pattern of public provision is needed in different areas. Priorities set at the centre for the country as a whole may not be sensible for individual regions. Some regions may require hospitals rather than schools, roads rather than housing. Or within specific programmes, one region may need new trunk roads and another significant improvements to existing roads, or more houses at a lower standard rather than fewer houses at a higher standard.

A number of the features of our present system are indicted as being responsible for this alleged lack of responsiveness to varying regional requirements. The system of decision-making at the centre is concerned with priorities within and between functional departments of state – housing, health, education and so on – on a basis of political judgements about the needs of Britain as a whole. Once these policy decisions have been made, resources are allocated to different areas on the basis of their educational, housing or health needs. It is argued that the pattern of expenditure and the policies on which it is based may make sense nationally, but the resulting, almost incidental pattern for particular areas is not necessarily sensible: people in the regions see this accidental pattern of expenditure to be often inappropriate to the real needs of the region. Put in another way (as Derek Senior describes), *vertical* decision-making within functional areas of policy is too strongly developed. What is required is a greater degree of comprehensive *horizontal* decision-making for territorial units through which all the peculiar needs of each territorial area can be more adequately comprehended. New governmental structures which were capable of assessing the needs of the North East as a whole, for example, might well produce a very different pattern of expenditure and very different public policy than the *ad hoc* amalgam of policies which had aimed at meeting the educational, health and housing needs of the region separately.

A further related feature of our present system which comes under attack is the degree of control over standards of provision exercised by central government. It is argued that this imposes an unwarranted uniformity throughout the country. Uniform standards for new house construction, school building or road construction, or for pupil–teacher ratios, for example, may remove a good deal of flexibility for dealing with the regions' real needs. If it was sensible for a region to build houses at a lower standard than Parker Morris in order to increase the scale of house-building, or in order to divert resources to other areas of policy such as the encouragement of industrial expansion, the present system would not allow this to happen. Moreover, the enforcement of uniform standards across a whole range of social provision results in detailed vetting of schemes by central government which not only slows up the process of actually completing those schemes on the ground, but slows up central government decision-taking too. It also diverts central government's attention away from its main job of laying down broad policy guide-lines in both domestic and foreign policy.

On those grounds, devolutionists suggest that national government could shed some of its powers to sub-national authorities, including power to fix public spending priorities within their areas and to depart, if they think fit, from national standards. This level should be the region, as it is only here that many of the necessary tasks can be performed, again in Derek Senior's terms, with 'functional efficiency'. Regions are the appropriate socio-geographical units for the making of broad allocative decisions and planning the future development of the area. Any unit smaller than a region, including local authority areas, is inappropriate, largely because the solution of many social and economic problems requires a larger spatial scale than local authority areas allow. Technological change, especially in the field of transportation, has united urban areas very closely with their rural hinterlands, which has created new patterns of work and leisure for city and country dwellers. The problems of decay in the old urban areas and growth in the wider metropolitan areas are intimately linked and can only be dealt with in a regional framework. Old urban areas, for example, cannot provide decent housing for all their inhabitants and have to look for land outside their boundaries. They may take the form of large new towns or cities as around London, or of large new developments such as Chelmsley Wood outside Birmingham. The need for a regional authority is made all the more urgent because local authorities cannot agree about the location and scale of population and employment growth or decline, and its associated social infrastructure. This issue is particularly pertinent in England as the boundaries of the reorganised local authorities, especially of the conurbation counties, are so tightly drawn that none of the major urban centres include within their boundaries their associated rural hinterland. The need for regional government in England, then, is strengthened by the creation in 1972 of an inadequate system of local government.

Besides being the appropriate unit for physical planning, the region is also seen as necessary for economic planning, especially in those regions which suffer from a declining employment base and poor environmental conditions. It is generally accepted that such regions, especially in the north of England, need new jobs and new infrastructure if they are to reduce high unemployment rates, low activity rates and out-migration, and catch up with the rest of Britain in terms of general prosperity. Central government regional policy has been an attempt to stimulate growth in these areas, and a number of studies (especially by Brown[7] and by Rhodes and Moore[8]) have shown it has achieved a fair measure of success. However, it has been suggested that regional government could take the process of economic planning much further in such regions. It could relate economic planning more closely to the physical planning of infrastructure, and, if given the power, could vary the levels of incentives given to industrialists to expand and modernise.[9] Again the argument is that the economic development of the poorer regions is best entrusted to local people who have greater knowledge of and commitment to the regions concerned.

Arguments about functional efficiency rest therefore on the proposition that the region is a spatial unit of *significance* in the making of public policy. Its significance has been growing and has been recognised largely in *ad hoc* institutions at regional level, whose activities are rarely co-ordinated. A regional government, under a scheme of devolution of power, could have the responsibility of examining the overall needs of the region in social, economic and physical terms, constructing medium- and long-term plans for meeting those needs and adjusting public expenditure and national standards accordingly. This would require them to take control over the activities of agencies now operating at regional level and to have power to co-ordinate the activities of local authorities, especially as regards land use and capital investment. Derek Senior describes in more detail how such a scheme would work.

Many of the points made so far could have been advanced, and indeed were, at any time over the past fifty years. However, more recent developments can be used to strengthen the case. Britain's economic future is fairly gloomy for the next few years at least, and a number of pundits see relatively little change thereafter. Economic growth is to be very slow; standards of living are to rise very little and public expenditure is to be held severely in check (hopefully). The last Public Expenditure white paper testifies to these forecasts.[10] If this is the case, it seems doubly important in the future to make wise decisions about public expenditure, to avoid waste and to use what public resources there are to the very best advantage. The devolutionists' case suggests that in the past our system of centralised decision-taking was spending money on projects which the regions did not need and neglecting projects which the regions did need. If public resources are to become scarcer, they could be better used if controlled by local people in the regions, who are the best judges of priorities.[11] Moreover, a slowing down of economic growth emphasises the need for Britain to develop its own indigenous and unused resources to the full. The underused men and women in areas of high unemployment constitute a significant element of those resources. If a case for greater regional autonomy in economic matters existed in the past, it can be argued that the prospect of the medium-term future must strengthen it.

A second development is the existence and influence of the EEC, assuming Britain remains a member. The Kilbrandon Report noted the growing control over certain economic and social policies exercised from Brussels, and in the long term this trend can be expected to continue. In operating these powers, especially in the field of regional policy and when attempting to bring about smooth adjustments to industrial change, the region can be seen as a much more sensible unit that the nation-state. The latter is too heterogeneous because, certainly in Britain's case, it masks significant spatial differences important for the operation of European economic policy. The nation-state can be a hindrance to the recognition of these differences in policy-making. Moreover, in the long run, having to operate on the basis of the nation-state might hinder the development of natural political alliances between regions with a common economic interest. In the European context, the North-West region of England may have more in common with Southern Italy or with Brittany than it has with the South East or the West Midlands in England.[12] The operation of European economic policy and the construction of political alliances on which it might be based would be helped by the creation of regional governments which reflected these important sub-national differences.

Again, a few comments on these arguments are appropriate here. First, they apply much more to the English regions than to Scotland and Wales. In the latter, the regional dimension has already been reflected in the secretary of state system, which to some degree has allowed the distinctiveness of those two areas to be recognised. Scotland too has had a local government reorganisation which created sub-regional authorities, especially around Glasgow, which unite town and country within common boundaries. As we have already noted, England's reorganisation often did just the opposite.

However, the regional dimension in England has not been totally neglected. There are a number of governmental institutions at regional level. Some of these relate to specific services and are examples of administrative decentralisation: Sir George Godber describes how the regional level was considered an essential element in the Health Service – the provision of specialised hospital services or the distribution of skilled manpower would be very difficult without it. Timothy Raison also shows how the provision of higher education has to have a regional element in it. Moreover, the need for a general co-ordinating capacity in both economic and social matters at regional level has also been recognised in the Economic Planning Boards of senior regional civil servants, and the Economic Planning Councils for which they work. More recently, strategic plans for a number of English regions have been undertaken which attempt to fulfil the comprehensive role for regional government outlined above.[13] Their terms of reference are to provide a framework within which local authorities should conduct their own long-term planning and to advise central government on what might be required on 'public expenditure, and economic and social policies relating to the regions' future development'.[14] Thus, they are moving towards the comprehensive examination of regional needs which Derek Senior advocates.

However, devolutionists would argue that these attempts at planning and co-ordination at regional level merely strengthen their case, and that their lack of success in influencing local or central government or the *ad hoc* regional institutions points to the next logical step, the creation of semi-autonomous regional government with real powers to implement the strategic plans. But the essential question is not so much what is decided but who decides. Who finally decides whether the South West has a spine road, or that the North West concentrates its new investments in the Liverpool–Manchester axis, or that East Anglia diverts some of its resources of money and manpower to the declining rural areas and market towns of north Norfolk? The devolutionists argue that, within broad limits, it should be those people living in the regions. Those against devolution assert that there is little alternative to letting central government have the final say.

THE CASE AGAINST REGIONAL DEVOLUTION

If the basis of the case for devolution involves values associated with a liberal version of democracy, the case against devolution rests on fundamental values about equality and equal citizenship. Historically speaking, as Marshall showed us,[15] the first step to equal citizenship was equality before the law; then followed equality of political rights, particularly through universal suffrage, and finally, although by no means complete, equalisation of social and economic opportunities as regards access to jobs, protection of family incomes, educational opportunities and so on. An essential element in achieving a degree of equality in social and economic opportunities was the progressive centralisation of public power. Narrow local oligarchies showed themselves both unable and unwilling to discharge their obligations in this respect: they had neither the resources nor the political desire to do so. Only the central government was able to impose basic and uniform standards throughout the country, to protect deprived minorities and, through its taxing capacities, to redistribute resources from rich to poor, whether they be people or areas. Those who hold that the prime aim of public policy should be to maintain and extend social and economic equality, are going to be suspicious of any attempt to seriously undermine the centralisation of power by schemes of regional devolution (although more limited forms of decentralisation might be acceptable). They maintain that some degree of diversity is both necessary and unavoidable, but that any reform which might lead to a widening of inequality is to be avoided.

This point of view is well represented in almost all the chapters in this book and therefore it need not be discussed at great length here. However, it may be useful to highlight one or two points. Expectations about social rights seem to be expanding rather than contracting. For example, while it is possible for most people now to accept the need for less inequality in access to educational opportunities or health care, over the last few years we have seen a new category of 'rights' emerging, concerned with the environment. David

Eversley implies that access to beautiful buildings, the countryside, pollution-free rivers and so on are basically a national, not a local, responsibility, because they are changing from desirable extras into inviolable opportunities which should be open to all. If this process of change continues (and there seems every likelihood that it will), then the scope for devolution could seem considerably less.

The period of economic difficulties ahead of us emphasises, in some people's view, the need to take from the rich regions and give to the poor, and this perhaps strengthens fears about the possibility of redistribution in a scheme of devolution. The absence of powerful regional governments in the past has meant that national resources could be distributed, in part at least, on an objective and egalitarian assessment of need. If regional government did exist, the distribution of resources from the centre would become, much more than now, a process of political horse-trading in which the political strength rather than the objective need of regions would play an important part. This criticism applies whether the resources involved are one-off major capital investments such as new public industrial plant, or general current and capital expenditures on improving the quality of various services such as health or education, or limited supplies of mobile jobs in the private sector. This might not be too serious in times of economic growth, but is serious when resources are scarce. Moreover, the creation of regional political institutions may create expectations in the regions which have little hope of being met, given slow economic growth. Diamond has argued that inter-regional conflicts could, even without regional government, be positively dangerous, and threaten cohesion and stability.[16] Furthermore, slow economic growth makes control over levels of public expenditure in the context of national economic management particularly important. Given the difficulties of controlling local authority expenditure, the creation of additional semi-autonomous spending authorities would not help.

These latter points relate to the inter-regional distribution of resources. David Eversley also raises the issue of intra-regional distribution of resources given regional government. A traditional role for central government has been to care for and protect minorities. If power over resource allocation was located at a local level, the weak bargaining position of minority groups in local political conflict would be exposed and the local majority could impose its will. Central government, as an outside power, has been prepared to step in and protect minority rights. Eversley, for example, raises the question of the inner city dweller, who in a regional context would form a small minority. He is not prepared to trust regional government to protect their interests: he asserts that the regional government would reflect real political power in each region and thus tend to maintain the *status quo*. There would be no real improvement for the inner city inhabitant if such improvement meant denying facilities to the richer suburbs, using the Green Belt as building land, or spending more on public housing to cater for the homeless.

A second disadvantage seen to flow from regional devolution concerns co-ordination, and the ability of government to deal with problems of externalities. It is necessary in policy-making to maintain links with a wide range of public and private bodies in order to ensure that public policies are not contradictory, that effort is not duplicated and that decisions are taken on the best possible basis of information. These linkages, and the adjustments of policy which flow from them, could be threatened by regional devolution. A. R. Isserlis, Timothy Raison and Sir George Godber are particularly concerned with this issue. They argue that central government departments gain a good deal from having executive responsibility for various policy areas. This ensures a feedback of information from local authorities and the general public which is vital for the ongoing development of policy. Schemes of devolution would severely limit this feedback, as executive responsibility would rest with regional authorities and it is they who would be the prime point of contact for local government and the public. This, they argue, would make it difficult for central government to lay down broad national policy, still less enforce it.

A further problem about co-ordination is raised by David Eversley. Some of the most important governmental decisions are about major investments such as the electrification of the railways, the need for new or expanded airports, the location of heavy industrial plant such as steel mills or oil-processing units. These are key decisions from which many other decisions about the location and scale of population and employment growth or social infrastructural investment naturally flow. If severe dislocation is to be avoided, these decisions can only be taken at a national level, since their effects are felt beyond the area, even region, in which they are located. For example, as Eversley argues, the decision to have a third London airport greatly affects the ability of Manchester and Liverpool to expand or maintain the level of traffic at their own airports. For major investment policy, therefore, there needs to be a high degree of co-ordination between agencies and between different parts of the country. Eversley points out that to the extent that these kinds of decisions have to remain at the centre, and given that other decisions basically flow from them, devolution of power to regions would be something of a sham, since the degree of real discretion would be very limited.

Another set of objections to devolution relate to doubts about its practical feasibility, especially during this decade. As we have already noted, proposals for creating a regional level of government followed hard on the heels of major organisational reform in many areas of policy, particularly the Health Service and local government. Such reorganisations cause a good deal of dislocation and it takes a considerable amount of time before those operating the system, both officials and elected members, have it working smoothly. Thus, there is likely to be a great deal of resistance from such people to the creation of a new layer of government, which, as Derek Senior demonstrates, will result in a new phase of disruption and adjustment. Part of the problem, as Sir George Godber points out in relation to health services, is that regional boundaries suitable for some purposes might not be appropriate for many other policy purposes. These arguments constituted one (though only one) of the reasons why, at the seminar which led to the production of this book, most of the senior government officials present showed strong sympathy with the case against devolution presented by A. R. Isserlis. Generally, it seems that support for devolution often comes from those who are very knowledgeable about, but have had little direct experience of actually operating, our system of government, and that the gravest doubts about devolution come from those who have had front-line experience of making the governmental machine work.

There is also a case for accepting local government reorganisation as an accomplished fact, and building on its strengths, rather than stressing its weaknesses. It could be wasteful to be diverted by the issue of regional devolution from the pressing job of improving relationships between central government and the new local authorities. The fact that the latter are slowly introducing corporate management principles provides the most realistic hope of obtaining the comprehensive assessment of needs which Derek Senior desires, for it is at the local authority level that decision-taking could break out of the straitjacket of the vertical, functional approach. Moreover, Timothy Raison argues that, at least for education, the existing relationship between national and local government produces a good deal of freedom and diversity at the local level. He suggests that such diversity may be eroded by regional governments, as the powers which the Memorandum of Dissent confers upon them would result in a degree of control over the activities of local education authorities far beyond that exercised now by central government.

A further practical problem is that even if, in England, it were decided to devolve government to regional authorities, there would be no obvious political leaders at regional level who could take over. The underlying argument here is that there needs to be clear political expression of regional feeling before devolution of power can take place: the issue of centralisation is side-stepped and the issue of political consciousness takes its place.

Finally, Kenneth Urwin and Timothy Raison emphasise the point that as far as personal social services and education are concerned, there is little need for a regional dimension at all. Both are services which are essentially local in character, and the local authority is a large enough unit for their effective operation. Indeed, Urwin argues that the local authority unit is almost too large; that the trend in personal social services is to decentralise into small neighbourhood units, and that it is there that the necessary co-ordination is most needed, in face-to-face contact with individuals in need, at the point of delivery rather than at the level of resource allocation and planning.

Derek Senior attempts to counter a number of these arguments in his chapter, but it may be valuable to add some points here. Arguments about the need to avoid further dislocation are no doubt important. Yet, simply on rational grounds, it would be unfortunate if the case for regional government should founder on the historical accident, partly caused by political impatience, that changes in the structure of local government and the health service were a *fait accompli* before the Kilbrandon Commission reported. Ideally, they should all have been considered together since they relate so closely to one another. Secondly, while it is true that there are no political movements based on common regional identity in England, political leadership did develop quite quickly in the new units created by local government reorganisation and some of *them* were very artificial in terms of popular loyalty and attachment. This is, in fact, something of a chicken-and-egg situation, for the creation of strong regional authorities may itself produce the political expression and popular attachment which is now lacking. Thirdly, the arguments of Timothy Raison and Kenneth Urwin about the importance of local delivery of services apply when a single service is looked at from within. However, they do not fully meet the case that it may still be at regional level that useful decisions can be taken about priorities *among* different services – whether to spend money on schools, or personal social services, or housing. Service delivery is one thing, but the devolutionists are more concerned about the planning of public policy, and it is here that the regional level is seen as being most important.

THE ARGUMENTS ASSESSED

The issue of regional devolution does arouse basic differences of value, around which all the more complex and subtle arguments and facts are organised. There is thus a temptation to see the issue in terms of irreconcilable dichotomies – equality or liberty; uniformity or diversity; democratic control or bureaucratic control; functional or territorial organisation of government. However, regional devolution illustrates very well the dilemmas and difficulties which arise from attempts to pursue multiple objectives. Governments want to achieve both equality *and* liberty, uniformity *and* diversity: each individually is seen as a legitimate objective. In practice then, the issue is not either/or, but what should be the appropriate balance or mix at a particular point in time.

This can be seen from the chapters in this book. Devolutionists like Derek Senior argue that the process of centralisation and bureaucratisation has gone too far and that it threatens liberty and diversity; what is needed is the movement of government power to separate centres of authority in the regions. They also agree, however, that not all functions can be devolved: Senior, for example, accepts the need for central government to redistribute resources, to lay down national guidelines, and to take major investment decisions. Anti-devolutionists like A. R. Isserlis also accept that decentralisation is needed; they agree that the region is an appropriate level to which decentralisation should take place, and that this has already been recognised by the creation of a number of regional institutions. The difference between them is partly one of degree. Derek Senior believes that liberty and diversity are important enough to warrant devolution of power to autonomous democratically elected governments; A. R. Isserlis believes it is more important to safeguard national priorities, standards and integrity, and that a stronger version of administrative decentralisation will be sufficient to meet the other desiderata.

The practical issue, then, is the degree to which the areal distribution of power in Britain should be changed, and all the arguments presented so far apply. However, there are other points which can be made here. The anti-devolutionist case accepts that local people, if given a fair degree of autonomy, cannot be trusted to pursue sufficiently egalitarian policies. Many might deny the validity of this statement in this form, yet it seems a reasonable conclusion to draw. This attitude is partly a product of history. David Eversley mentions the inadequacy and corruption of local oligarchies in the vestry system and the need progressively to erode local powers of autonomy. The assumption is that if powers were devolved and the process of centralisation reversed, the same problems could re-emerge. However, is it reasonable to assume that a process which was required to *create* a system based on values of equality of social and economic opportunity, is also necessary to *maintain* it? The process itself has changed the situation considerably. Whatever the inadequacies of British society at the moment, beliefs associated with Malthus and the Poor Law are no longer dominant, largely because individuals have been socialised by a society in which a considerable reduction of inequality of social and economic opportunity has in fact been occurring steadily. This does not imply total consensus, but it does suggest a firm enough basis for hoping that any variations arising from regional devolution would in practice be within acceptable limits. In short, the very process of centralisation in the past, and the changes in beliefs and attitudes associated with it, may by now have created the conditions in which the reverse process could be allowed to take place.

A further plank in the anti-devolutionist case is that central government must have the power to redistribute resources from the rich to the poor. In the development of social policy over the last decade or so, one variation on this theme has been the concept of positive discrimination: that is, a view which accepts that normal redistributive measures in the pursuit of equality are not enough, and that the special needs of certain deprived groups or areas require extra resources over and above normal allocations. This idea has taken a practical form largely in small-area policies such as the Educational Priority Areas, the Urban Programme, or Community Development Projects. The amounts of money concerned have usually been small, and the policies have been criticised on those grounds.[17] They have commonly been applied to small capital projects, environmental improvement, or the injection of additional skilled manpower. However, a further resource is political power and, as in the United States, this is also reflected in our own small-area policies where there is a strong emphasis on citizen participation and the creation of political muscle in deprived communities.

It can be argued that positive discrimination in the form of extra political opportunities has existed in our formal system of government for some time, at the regional level. This is seen in the special arrangements for Scotland and Wales. Both have had, for varying amounts of time, separate administrative arrangements and separate political representation in the persons of the Secretaries of State in the British Cabinet. The oral evidence given to the Kilbrandon Commission by officials at the Scottish and Welsh Offices indicated that these arrangements might well have given the two areas a special advantage in Whitehall and Westminster when questions of resource allocation were being decided.[18] Sir George Godber in his chapter suggests that, as far as health is concerned, the separate political voice of these two areas has indeed resulted in extra resources being allocated to them, even though the case was just as strong for a number of English regions.

This special advantage to Wales and Scotland was no doubt acceptable partly because of their cultural distinctiveness, but also, and more importantly here, because they were relatively poor and underdeveloped regions. They displayed many of the characteristics of economically backward regions described earlier. However, a number of English regions are very similar in character, especially the three northern regions – Yorkshire and Humberside, the North West, and the Northern region. Indeed this has been recognised also in special political arrangements – at least for the Northern region. Lord Hailsham, with a seat in the Cabinet, was made Minister for the North East in the Macmillan administration in the early 1960s, to cope with the pressing economic difficulties facing that region.

These arguments suggest that regional decentralisation on a selective basis to the poorer regions of Britain can be seen as a highly specialised form of positive discrimination and could be justified on these grounds. But it would have to be selective in order to operate in this way. A major reason why Wales and Scotland obtained special help was because their separate political arrangements were the exception, not the rule. If all the regions of Britain had had a similar arrangement, Wales and Scotland might well have lost their distinctive advantage. This can be used to counter Sir George Godber's suggestion (discussed also by Derek Senior) that regional devolution might work towards a better distribution of health service funds in England.

It is of course impossible, as Randall has indicated, to disprove the assertion that Scotland and Wales would have received extra help anyway, without the existence of the Secretaries of State, purely on the basis that they needed it most.[19] However, looking at regional decentralisation in this way tends to break down a number of rigidities in the argument. For one thing, it casts doubt on the assumption, both in the Kilbrandon Report and some chapters in this book, that there must be one solution applied uniformly to all the English regions. Stanyer has pointed out that one purpose of decentralisation is to reflect and encourage differences between areas: if the areas are indeed different, they may require different forms of treatment.[20] The distinction advocated here would be between the rich regions and poor regions, and it may be that one practical approach to devolution would be to recognise these differences, within a united kingdom. In this case, Scotland and Wales would not be divided from England on the basis of their different culture and political history, but they would be viewed, along with the three northern regions of England, as areas needing special political arrangements because of their special economic and social characteristics. Such an approach would also soften the dichotomy between equality and liberty, since selective regional decentralisation, while producing more liberty in the political sense, may also produce greater equality by extracting extra resources in bargaining with Whitehall and Westminster.

We can now turn to another set of issues. So far the problem has been discussed in terms of alternative forms of decentralisation. However, are there solutions to the problems raised by the devolutionists, other than devolution itself? Is the diagnosis right, but the prescription wrong? One of the devolutionists' arguments is that government is not responsive to the real needs of people because it is too remote, being concentrated to a high degree at the centre. In one sense, their solution is to introduce market principles into the organisation of government. Instead of having almost a monopoly, eight to ten new arms of government would be created through the break-up of that monopoly. Each would be free, within limits, to provide what it thought best, and people in theory would be able to choose which area to live in according to their preferences. The variety of provision and policy would act to stimulate change and experimentation, which could be adopted by other regional governments if it proved successful.

However, if we are interested in making government more responsive to people's needs, one alternative is to go a stage further and introduce market principles more fully. This could be done by charging consumers at the point of consumption for a large range of services now provided by government; or by reducing the government's role in the provision of certain services altogether, leaving it up to the economic market to provide them. This approach has been consistently advocated by the Institute of Economic Affairs, and their views about charging full economic cost for government-produced goods and services, and the introduction of voucher schemes for services such as education, are well known.[21] The economic market-place would be responsive to people's preferences, as expressed through their willingness or unwillingness to buy (even though not everyone has the same opportunity to enter it, given the unequal distribution of income). These views are probably extreme, but they do suggest that one alternative to devolution, given that the problem is the responsiveness of government to people's needs and preferences, may be to concentrate more on increasing money incomes generally, especially at the bottom end of the scale. This might give individuals a greater opportunity to choose and express their preferences than policies which concentrate on providing goods and services in kind.

Secondly, we raised the question earlier in this introduction that if the democratic benefits of devolution were going to be purely psychological, were there other ways of achieving them? The last few years have perhaps shown that some of the democratic benefits which are hoped for from devolution are already being produced by two developments: the growth of pressure groups in all fields of public policy, and the movement towards 'client' participation in some of our institutions, such as schools, factories and housing estates. A major purpose of constitutional reform as seen by the Kilbrandon Commissioners was to be the restoration of public confidence in the democratic process. Their main method was to restructure the areal distribution of power and to increase the power of directly-elected members. They wished to see greater opportunity for individuals to become councillors (or regional assemblymen). They were concerned with the *formal and traditional* aspects of democracy – central and local relationships, political parties, voting procedures, the relationship between the legislature and the executive.

There is an understandable tendency for people to attach ideological commitment to institutional forms as well as to social purposes, which can perhaps lead to a tendency to try to adapt existing institutions to do jobs of which they are incapable in changed circumstances. This may be the case with our formal system of democratic government. One important development over the last decade has been the growth of pressure groups of various kinds outside government. These are both national and local in character, and they cover the whole spectrum of public policy from Claimants' Unions on the one hand to amenity and preservation societies on the other. A number of reasons have been put forward for their growth: for example, rising living standards, greater educational opportunities, and the mass media, are seen as increasing awareness and self-respect.[22] It is through participation in the activities of such groups that many citizens are exercising their democratic freedoms, rather than through political parties and the formal democratic system. Moreover, political parties and the elected representative system, by their nature, often cannot cater for this. Many pressure groups are concerned with specific, often short-term, local issues which do not relate easily to party ideologies or policies. Even in local government, elected representatives often have to take an 'overall view' of issues and cannot speak solely in the interests of their constituents.[23] Moreover, constituencies are very large (a regional assemblyman, for instance, would on average represent 80–90,000 people) and there are relatively few councillors anyway. The addition of an extra hundred elected members for each region is not going to increase opportunities enormously.

The growth of these groups has partly brought about changes in the processes of decision-taking which are aimed at making government more open and responsive – consultation procedures in structure and local planning, and in transport planning, neighbourhood councils, citizen involvement in General Improvement Area schemes, Community Health Councils in the Health Service, and local government green papers. It could be argued that the growth of pressure groups has already produced a degree of decentralisation of real power and has forced government at all levels to be more responsive to people's wishes, and that an extension of changes similar to those described above could be an alternative to changes in the formal structure of power.

The same conclusion can also be drawn from a second trend. This is the attempts of people to become involved with specific institutions of which they are an integral part. These are not pressure groups attempting to influence government from the outside, but clients, employees or customers who are a basic part of the institution itself. Examples would be worker participation in factories and businesses, parent and pupil participation in schools, or tenants' associations in public housing estates.[24] Such activities may be able to make a much greater contribution to reducing feelings of powerlessness and encouraging active interest and involvement, than regional devolution. Such participation draws directly on people's knowledge and experience; the institutions concerned touch on the immediate interests of most people – the home, children and work. This form of participatory involvement may have an important part to play in reinterpreting democracy in the 1970s and 1980s.

These arguments lead one step further. Perhaps our concern with making changes in the formal structure of government is diverting attention away from the real problems. David Eversley argues that serious economic failure over the past thirty years, allied with inadequate redistributive mechanisms, is the cause of a wide range of problems in Britain – high unemployment, poor housing performance, ugly central city redevelopment and so on. It is issues such as these which are at the root of much discontent and dissatisfaction, and their solution lies in increasing economic growth and distributing its product more equitably. While regional government may have some part to play here, this achievement will depend on measures other than redistributing powers from one level of government to another.

THE ALTERNATIVES FOR ENGLAND

On the basis of the arguments presented so far, we can now sketch out some of the alternatives for England. In its discussion document in early 1974,[25] and in its White Paper of September 1974,[26] the government concentrated attention on Scotland and Wales. Besides commenting that there had not been very great pressure for substantial devolution in England, the White Paper stated that there would have to be a good deal of further consultation in England before it was clear 'what the people of England want'.[27] In the debate on the White Paper in February 1975, Mr Edward Short hoped that 'we may begin, later this year, consultations in the English regions such as we had in both Scotland and Wales in the summer of last year.'[28] The government's view seemed to be, therefore, that England was a much less urgent case than Scotland or Wales, and that all the options were open, although the English regions would receive nothing *more* than Scotland and Wales, and probably less.

The first alternative is to opt for *no change*. This does not rule out the occasional case of administrative decentralisation, or the commissioning of further strategic regional plans, or further co-operation of local authorities in providing certain services. However, these changes would occur naturally in the course of time as and when the need arose. This option therefore sees the possibility of the creation of *ad hoc* regional institutions for specific purposes much as in the past. Kenneth Urwin mentions the possibility of greater co-ordination between authorities in providing for the homeless, especially in London. Timothy Raison suggests that there may be a case for strengthening the Regional Councils for Further Education. Within his option too come the proposals, set out in the Strategic Plans for the North West and the South East, for having permanent teams of professionals in a regional planning unit to provide advice to central and local government about policy changes in the light of changing regional circumstances. Certainly these are new developments, but, like similar developments in the past, are marginal and incremental. This option accepts that the arguments about practical feasibility are on balance decisive, at least until and unless genuine regional political movements developed on any significant scale One of the difficulties here is that the creation of further un-coordinated, unaccountable regional institutions might in the long run strengthen the case for co-ordinating them and making them accountable: a no-change strategy in the short term may increase pressures for significant change in the long term.

The second option is to undertake a further phase of *limited local government re-organisation*. Derek Senior argues strongly in his paper that the need for regional government springs partly from an ill-considered reform of local government in 1972. The adoption of his ideas for local authorities based on city-regions, or even Redcliffe-Maud's proposals for unitary authorities, would have created local government units large enough and powerful enough almost to preclude the need for strong regional authorities now. As things stand, many boundaries – especially those for the conurbation authorities – make little sense in socio-economic terms, and important functions, especially in planning and housing matters, are the responsibility of the district authorities, which are too small to exercise them effectively. One possibility therefore would be to unscramble the whole local government system, or at least to undertake a more limited reform around the large conurbations, in which some powers would be removed from the districts to the counties, and the boundaries of the latter adjusted to fit socio-economic reality rather better. Effective corporate planning would seem more likely if these changes took place. However, this could be achieved without any significant devolution of power from central government. It may be that this strengthened system of local government could be given more discretion in some respect *vis-à-vis* Whitehall, but the fundamental relationship between central and local government would not change.

A third alternative is for a thorough-going scheme of *administrative decentralisation*. The details of one such scheme are set out in A. R. Isserlis' chapter. National government in Whitehall would be considerably slimmed down, and its presence in the regions would be considerably enlarged, up to and beyond the level it has already reached in Scotland and Wales. Departments which now have little or no regional presence, such as the Treasury, would, under this scheme, have to take part. The regional civil service, and perhaps regional ministers, would be exposed to the advice and stimulus of strengthened regional consultative councils or assemblies. The maximum discretion would be allowed to the regional structure, consistent with the meeting of national ministerial responsibility. Devices such as block allocation of public expenditure would be used within this general framework, and this would mean changes in the way central government undertakes public expenditure planning: functional, departmental needs would give way to some degree to territorial needs. In this way, much of the *exercise* of power would be moved to the regions, even though the possession and direction of that power would remain at the centre.

Fourthly, there are proposals for *executive devolution.*

Such a scheme would invest powers in a democratically elected assembly, which would have final say over a wide range of matters. It would be a comprehensive level of government, being empowered to act across almost the whole field of public policy. Derek Senior describes in some detail the functions of such bodies, and also suggests ways in which their operations may be financed. Thus their own exclusive tax base might be taxation on private motoring (vehicle duty, petrol tax and driving-licence fees) and the yield arising from the public acquisition of development land at existing use value and its sale at market value. Senior describes how such authorities would take over responsibility for all existing regional institutions of government; would have control over the capital investment programme of local authorities, and eventually take over some of their planning powers. He also raises the issue of the boundaries of the new regional authorities and suggests ways of defining them which would create spatial units appropriate to all the functions which regional authorities would need to perform. One consequence of this scheme, as he sees it, is that it may lead to a fairly radical change in the structure of local government: there would no longer be any need for two levels of administration below the region, and a single local government tier would then be a possibility.

A limited variation of this alternative has been put forward by the team which produced the strategic plan for East Anglia.[29] They suggest that there is a need for a regional institution which can undertake a comprehensive examination of the region's needs and be able to co-ordinate the activities of all executive agencies in the region so that those needs are met. The agency should have effective powers of sanction over the forward programmes of these executive bodies (which basically means their capital programmes), and it should have discretionary powers, together with financial resources to make those discretionary powers effective. The discretionary powers relate to matters which lie outside the responsibility of the specialised agencies, or result from changes and events which have not been foreseen. The size of the regional development fund available to the agency would be based on a percentage precept on the expenditure levels of all public bodies represented at the regional level. The body would not, however, be directly elected as in Senior's scheme, but would consist of representatives of all the major executive agencies in the region (presumably appointed by the Secretary of State for the Environment).

A fifth option is *selective regional decentralisation*. The justification for this has been described in the last section. The form of decentralisation could be either administrative decentralisation as A. R. Isserlis describes it, or executive devolution. A good deal of discussion would be needed about the precise basis for selecting regions, but *a priori* the three northern regions seem most appropriate. An essential feature of this scheme is to provide a *stronger* form of decentralisation for the selected regions than that applying elsewhere. One problem with this scheme is that, if it were successful in directing resources to the selected regions, the pressures for similar treatment coming from the other regions would be increased. Also, the more successful the scheme was in fulfilling its intentions of diverting resources, the stronger the case for removing their extra advantage. This suggests that the form of decentralisation here needs to be perhaps more flexible than a full scheme of executive devolution would allow. One possibility therefore might be to undertake administrative decentralisation to all regions, but to have regional ministers only for the selected regions.

These alternatives are not, of course, mutually exclusive. For example, one could reorganise local government around the conurbations (including London), and at the same time introduce administrative decentralisation in all regions. Legislative devolution does not seem a practical proposition for the English regions so long as they lack highly developed political consciousness.

The alternatives to formal structural change mentioned in the last section – the encouragement of market principles, and the extension of opportunities for participation by pressure groups and in organisations – have not been developed any further here. However, they are reasonable and realistic alternatives to the changes outlined above, if one is prepared to take a rather wider view of the issues than is usual.

The reader will not have found this introduction, nor will he find the pages which follow, full of hard factual evidence based on empirical research. Part of the explanation is that not a great deal of appropriate work has been done. Perhaps more important, the concepts and problems involved do not lend themselves to 'scientific' verification We have had to deal with elusive attributes such as feelings of powerlessness in the face of government, dissatisfaction with the way public affairs are conducted, the inefficiency of central government in conducting its business. Even if it were possible to obtain good measures of these attributes, their interpretation and explanation would be exceedingly difficult. Certainly, it must have been inspiration rather than anything else which enabled some of the Royal Commissioners to conclude that feelings of powerlessness and dissatisfaction which existed could only be dissipated by the creation of regional governments. Moreover, a good deal of the discussion is of the 'what if' variety, i.e. what would be the effects of making a particular change compared with what might have happened if the change had not been made. These sorts of questions become all the more indeterminate because we are dealing with large slices of our system of government, or the system as a whole, rather than with small and specific parts of it. We have already noted, too, that these issues turn on basic value judgements, and perhaps prejudices as well. Thus the basis of any case, whatever the factual superstructure, is often untestable. Perhaps this is one reason why many people fall back on political expression as the one true and obvious test of the need for regional devolution.

The authors of the various chapters have each reached their own individual conclusions on the issues and it would be inappropriate for this introduction to present any firm conclusion about the desirability or otherwise of regional devolution. However, it is legitimate to point out that England cannot be neglected if the problem is defined as the historical centralisation of political power in Britain; that the issue raises once again the dichotomy between the need for equality in social and economic opportunity, and the need for liberty and diversity; and that we must be prepared to face the real costs which regional devolution would entail for the continuing operation of both national and local government.

NOTES AND REFERENCES

1 Speech by W. E. Gladstone on 26 November 1879, in Dalkeith: quoted in P. Magnus, *Gladstone* (John Murray, 1963).

2 J. S. Mill, 'On Liberty', in *Utilitarianism, Liberty, Representative Government*, ed. H. B. Acton (J. M. Dent and Son, 1972) p. 68.
3 Royal Commission on the Constitution, *Devolution and Other Aspects of Government: An Attitudes Survey*, Research Paper 7 (HMSO, 1973).
4 For a description of some of these regional institutions in England see the *Kilbrandon Report*, ch. 7, and the *Memorandum of Dissent*, ch. 5.
5 For a discussion of some of the relevant issues, see J. K. Galbraith, *The New Industrial State* (André Deutsch, 1972); N. Harris, *Competition and the Corporate State* (Methuen, 1972); A. Shonfield, *Modern Capitalism: the Changing Balance of Public and Private Power* (Oxford University Press, 1965).
6 R. E. Pahl and J. Winkler, 'The Coming of Corporatism', *New Society* (10 Oct 1974) 72–6.
7 A. J. Brown, *The Framework of Regional Economics in the UK* (Cambridge University Press, 1972).
8 B. C. Moore and J. Rhodes, 'Evaluating the Effects of British Regional Economic Policy', *Economic Journal*, 83, no. 329 (Mar 1973) 87–110.
9 For a discussion of these points see M. Gaskin, *Centre and Region in Regional Policy*, paper given to Regional Policy and Planning Seminar, 28–30 September 1973, University of East Anglia.
10 *Public Expenditure to 1978–79*, Cmnd. 5879 (HMSO, 1975).
11 'The proportion of the population living in urban areas nationally is much greater than that in East Anglia, and as a consequence national priorities do not always fit the regional situation without adjustment. The possibilities for adjustment to secure a more effective use of scarce resources are limited. There would seem therefore, to be grounds for developing some form of intermediate mechanism which would allow regional priorities to be more clearly recognised . . .', *Strategic Choice for East Anglia* (HMSO, 1975) p. 125.
12 See, for example, P. E. Mayo, *The Roots of Identity* (Allen Lane, 1974).
13 This comprehensive approach is best seen in *The Strategic Plan for the North West* (HMSO, 1974) and *Strategic Choice for East Anglia*, and will probably be developed even further in the plan for the Northern region which is now in progress.
14 *Strategic Plan for the North West*, p. 268.
15 T. H. Marshall, 'Citizenship and Social Class', in *Sociology at the Crossroads* (Heinemann, 1963).
16 D. Diamond, *The Long Term Aim of Regional Policy*, paper given to Regional Policy and Planning Seminar, 28–30 September 1973, University of East Anglia.
17 See, for example, M. Meacher, 'The Politics of Positive Discrimination', in *Positive Discrimination and Inequality*, ed. H. Glennester and S. Hatch, Fabian Research Series 314.
18 Royal Commission on the Constitution, *Minutes of Evidence I: Wales*, pp. 8–16, 91–115; and *Minutes of Evidence II: Scotland*, pp. 2–48.

19 P. J. Randall, 'Wales in the Structure of Central Goverment', *Public Administration*, 50 (autumn 1972) 353–72.
20 J. Stanyer, 'Nationalism, Regionalism and the British System of Government', *Social and Economic Administration*, 8, no. 2 (summer 1974) 136–57.
21 The relevant documents are too numerous to list separately. They are published by the IEA largely in its Occasional Papers and Hobart Papers Series. For an interesting left-wing comment on them, see D. Collard, *The New Right: A Critique*, Fabian Tract 387.
22 See, for example, A. Arblaster, 'Participation: Context and Conflict', in *Participation in Politics*, ed. G. Parry (Manchester University Press, 1972) pp. 41–58; C. Pateman, *Participation and Democratic Theory* (Cambridge University Press, 1970); A. W. Benn, *The New Politics*, Fabian Tract 402.
23 J. G. Davies, *The Evangelistic Bureaucrat; a study of a planning exercise in Newcastle-upon-Tyne* (Tavistock Publications, 1972); and R. Batley, 'An Explanation of Non-Participation in Planning', *Policy and Politics*, I, no. 2 (Dec 1972) 95–114.
24 For a description of participation in some of these institutions see S. Hatch (ed.), *Towards Participation in Local Services*, Fabian Tract 419.
25 *Devolution within the United Kingdom: Some Alternatives for Discussion* (HMSO, 1974).
26 *Democracy and Devolution: Proposals for Scotland and Wales*, Cmnd. 5732 (HMSO, 1974).
27 Ibid., para. 25.
28 *Hansard, House of Commons*, vol. 885, no. 59, col. 957.
29 *Strategic Choice for East Anglia*, p. 125.

1 Regional Devolution and Environmental Planning

DAVID EVERSLEY

INTRODUCTION

The purpose of this chapter is to examine the scope for devolution of powers from central government to regional authorities in the field of environmental planning. It is not proposed, for this purpose, to re-examine the great majority of the topics which the Kilbrandon Commission regarded as essential elements in the present situation and which led them to come to the conclusions which were published at the end of 1973. They were concerned principally about the growth in the volume of government activity and its increasing complexity, dissatisfaction with the remoteness of the London decision-making process, and the rise of a new nationalism. Nor is it necessary to discuss again the merits of the various patterns of separatism, federalism, and partial devolution which have been canvassed on political or functional grounds. We can take it for granted that any constitutional reform resulting in the emergence of regional government, whether only in Scotland and Wales or also in the English regions, will include some form of financial provision which will continue to attempt to equalise living standards by redistributing revenues both on capital and on current account.[1] We may also take it for granted that any new authority created would dispose of its own civil service, and that legislative assemblies for Scotland and Wales would have the type of powers which are outlined in the Kilbrandon Report in Chapter 24. Significant powers would also be devolved, but more widely, under the scheme of executive devolution to the English regions advocated by Lord Foot and Sir James Steel,[2] quite apart from the even wider plan of devolution which was the subject of the Memorandum of Dissent.

In other words, this chapter will not attempt to open up again the debates which have exercised our collective minds for the last five years, and which have probably been closed for the time being by the transition into an age of non-action or at least minimum action, imposed on us by economic and political rather than functional considerations. If we leave aside these issues, then, the question can be posed thus: how far can decisions about land use and transportation planning, about environmental protection and settlement patterns, both as to capital spending and current expenditure, and as to administrative processes (e.g. development control), be left to whatever form of regional government may emerge, as opposed to being reserved to central government determination?

The present position is fairly clear. All legislation issues from Parliament in London, whether we are speaking of public general acts, acts with local (e.g. Scottish) applicability, or private acts. Although statutory obligations are imposed on all local authorities, there also exist a wide range of powers which Parliament makes available to local agencies (and the word here includes such bodies as the new health and water authorities, as well as *ad hoc* bodies like development corporations). All decisions taken under such legislation are subject to the normal control processes familiar in all fields of public activity: money to pay current charges may only be raised in ways approved by Parliament, and spent subject to public audit; loans to pay for capital development may only be raised with central government sanction, whether or not its participation is required. The actions of all authorities are the responsibility of a departmental minister whether in a general way (i.e. the Secretary of State for the Environment who is the successor of the Minister of Local Government) or on account of particular departmental functions (Education, Employment, Health and Social Security, Trade and Industry). Although this applies to all executive decisions, one particular class of such decisions, i.e. those relating to land-use planning and development, is subject to a special procedure which leads back to the Secretary of State in a more direct line: all planning decisions may be appealed against, and are subject to public inquiry under various procedures, which leave the Department as the final arbiter. Contrary to the widely held view, the new planning system of structure and local plans, though it involves fewer ministerial adjudications, is just as much subject to final central determination of disputed decisions as the previous development plan system. Although attempts are being made to streamline these procedures, the principle of central autonomy has not been seriously questioned.

Therefore the question is not whether this existing general system should be abrogated, but whether there are, in the field of environmental planning, a range of *final* decisions which could be the prerogative of an elected regional authority, or a body which exercises executive powers devolved from the centre without being controlled by an elected council. We stress the word *final* because, without such finality, devolution has no real meaning. There are of course many hundreds of thousands of decisions taken every year by levels of authority down to the parish councils which never reach the eyes and ears of Whitehall. But in every case the acceptance of such a decision by the parties affected rests on the presumption that the outcome is in accordance both with national legislation, and with a more local plan, resolution or budget which depends in turn for its legality on conformity with statutory rules. Let us illustrate the meaning of such a change in our system of government by reference to examples of particular classes of decision-making. These are chosen to illustrate the variety of principles which might be involved.

STANDARDS

We can distinguish two types of standards in the field of environmental planning: one which might be termed *absolute*, and the other which we might call *financially conditional.* Absolute standards are those which relate, for instance, to the duties of medical officers of health in representing housing as unfit; to a wide variety of public health engineering works; to road safety and lighting, and to water and aerial pollution Financially conditional standards are those which determine government grants or subsidies, such as those relating to the provision of new housing, (e.g. the application of the housing cost yardstick), principal road construction, clean air, countryside management and access, historic buildings and townscape, etc. Devolution would mean different things in the two cases. Where absolute standards are concerned, we might for instance consider the possibility that a regional authority would decide, on social or economic grounds, to instruct medical officers of health not to represent housing as unfit on the grounds that people in, say, Sunderland or Newcastle-upon Tyne, do not judge their traditional habitations on criteria applicable in Esher or Solihull.[3] A regional authority might prefer industry to operate profitability rather than incur unnecessary expenses by conforming to emission or effluent standards laid down nationally.

Where financially conditional standards are concerned, regional government might decide that Parker Morris standards are excessive for new building and what is required is a great deal of new semi-permanent housing quickly and cheaply. One region might decide that only full-size motorways would attract industry on the scale required; another might, on environmental grounds, prefer a system of partial trunk-road improvements, dualling and by-passes.

In practice it will be noted that decision-making, centralised as it is, is not now a matter either of simple imposition of specific duties on local authorities, or of continuous head-on clashes between local and central government either on matters of principle or of application. Thus, the housing yardstick is often quoted as an unnecessary central intervention in a matter of local policy. If a council wishes to build houses quickly, it may have to buy an expensive piece of land and accept a tender for construction which will result in a final cost, per dwelling, in excess of what the Department of the Environment is prepared to allow (because it is the Department which will foot the bill for the deficit that is produced). Although the operation of the yardstick is often put forward as a reason why London local authorities in particular have apparently been unable to achieve their housing targets, in practice several authorities have managed to build dwellings at costs greatly in excess of the yardstick and have received retrospective sanction, while the cost levels themselves have been frequently revised in answer to local pressures. The daily exchange of information, orders, appeals, complaints, interventions by MP's and ministerial replies amounts, in total, to a functioning of a system of delegation of responsibility. It is very rare indeed for the ultimate sanction of a surcharge, for instance, on local authority members or officers to be invoked.[4] Some commentators would say that this proves that the local authority normally defers to the views of central government; but alternatively, it could also be argued that the fact that so few councillors feel obliged to go to such lengths as the defiant members of the Clay Cross Urban District Council, who would not apply the government's rent legislation, only proved that in practice the system is flexible enough. Certainly one has ample evidence of the fact that both permissive legislation and mandatory rules are interpreted in widely different ways by local authorities.

Although the listing of buildings and the various types of conservation order now in operation are primarily a matter for the local authority, there are large categories of environmental decisions reserved to the central government, ranging from the protection of historic monuments to the designation of areas of outstanding natural beauty.[5] Mere listing or drawing of lines on maps is not of itself an important activity, but it is when any change of use is at issue (demolition of a listed building, a caravan site on a coastal stretch, access to a nature reserve) that reference to the central government is automatic. The point here is that we are essentially talking about matters of *judgement*, or taste, and here the divergence between national and regional standards may be considerable. There is no suggestion that such a divergence would be in one direction: regional authorities might be more or less jealous guardians of the 'national' heritage than Whitehall; they might be more or less disposed to sacrifice traditional amenities for the sake of tourist traffic, and so on. At present local opinion is regarded as largely irrelevant by the central Department. The phases of conservation-mindedness, starting with the preoccupation with prehistoric and Roman remains which prevailed fifty years ago, down to the current predilection for Victoriana and industrial archaeology, are reflected in central legislation and statutory orders. There are instances, of course, where sections of local opinion may be deemed to have prevailed over others (e.g. in the case of the Central Wales National Park), but in any case the decision is the Secretary of State's prerogative.

Yet here too we clearly have a two way traffic of consultation. Apart from the existence of separate historic buildings councils, for instance, for England, Wales and Scotland, the machinery for the safeguarding of structures ensures that the view of the local authority is heard in cases of dispute. The designation of every kind of special area, from nature reserves to coastal footpaths, depends on the active participation of the county planning authority. The machinery for the designation (and closure) of footpaths is a local matter even if the machinery is national in origin. The central government, in fact, only shows the extent of its powers in cases of dispute. It is quite common for a local authority to submit, for instance, a town-centre redevelopment plan, acting in conjunction with a developer. A local amenity society then objects to the plan, an inquiry is held, and the Secretary of State upholds the objectors (as in the case of the proposed redevelopment of the market in Chesterfield, not to speak of Covent Garden). Therefore one has to identify, in this field, conflicts of interest, where it is not a matter of local versus national government, but rather a state of dispute between rival interest groups, one of which may be an elected body, leaving the central government, after all, as the final arbiter of taste, utility and social advantage.

THE TECHNOLOGY OF THE ENVIRONMENT

Another important class of decisions relates to those, usually relatively expensive and indivisible, projects which, though often of primarily regional significance, involve the national government both as the principal source of finance and as the technical co-ordinator with developments in other regions. A few examples will suffice: airport policy (both on the question of a third London airport and its alleged substitute, a regional airport policy); energy policy (ranging from the Selby drift mine to decisions about types and siting of nuclear power stations, oil and natural gas production and distribution, and conventional power stations); railway policy (including electrification and retention of branch lines); water resources policy (which may be allied to other fields, e.g. in the case of the suggested estuarial barrages); and a ports policy. In each of these cases there have been a series of national inquiries, commissions, standing committees, expenditure committee investigations, etc. which recommended (or failed to recommend) policies with important regional implications.

Again some specific examples may be useful. The Third London Airport was first discussed in the early 1960s, when Stansted was chosen.[6] Local objections led to the appointment of the Roskill Commission, which recommended Cublington in Buckinghamshire. Sir Colin Buchanan, in a dissenting report, chose Foulness (Maplin) which was the site adopted by the central government. Local people in south-east Essex and north Kent bitterly opposed this decision; some economists and aircraft operators were also against the scheme. In 1974, Maplin was quietly abandoned and without further consultation the government embarked on a policy of increasing the capacity of Gatwick and, after all, Stansted, to tide the region over the next ten years at least. In due course, fresh opposition appeared (from the people living round Stansted and Gatwick), while any pretence at a regional, let alone national, airport strategy was abandoned. Decisions about the expansion of settlements close to the airports, and about the development of road and railway systems meanwhile continued to be made in a planning vacuum, with each local authority or statutory undertaker aiming to maximise their own gains in *ad hoc* investment decisions.[7] Therefore, though the fact that the ultimate power to build another national airport rests with central government, the existence of such indivisible linkages does not of itself guarantee a comprehensible and effective method of planning. The mere rescinding of a decision, or postponement of a plan, does not constitute a planning system.

The long history of the Channel tunnel is another case in point. Such a project, from its English end in Kent by way of access roads and rail tracks, to the London passenger terminal, can only be planned and financed centrally. However, the project aroused a great deal of local opposition (especially from people threatened by a high-speed railway line and those living round the proposed west London terminal); the economic climate was not considered ripe for such an undertaking, and finally the decision was taken to abandon the project, and to allow cross-channel traffic to grow in an unplanned fashion, that is to say, through the efforts of a dozen competing sea and air carriers operating from as many airfields and harbours.

Thus it is usually only when a major investment decision is finally translated into action that the hegemony of the central government produces a whole series of linked decisions in which local authorities cannot then play a very important part. The development of the North Sea gas and oil fields is an illustration of this. Although gas was first brought ashore in Norfolk, this had few environmental or economic repercussions. It was the decision, in 1968, to bring practically all the oil from the known fields ashore in Scotland which materially altered both the inter-regional balance of advantage, and the local planning system in Scotland. It was decided, in the interests of regional policy, to land all oil in Scotland, though as a proportion of the total cost of production, the undersea pipelines are a relatively insignificant part compared to the drilling rigs and shore installations. Had central government decided, in 1968, to bring some of the oil into the Tyne and Tees areas, this might have both provided an important economic stimulus to the Northern region, and avoided the delicate political situation in which a possible Scottish monopoly of oil production has reinforced the demand for independence. As it is, the imbalance of economic advantage now exists within Scotland itself; attempts to allow some of the western coastal areas to have some of the financial benefits from construction work having foundered on the rock of environmental protection. But is should be noted that the total effect of the North Sea oil policy has been a more profound transformation of a large tract of Scottish countryside than had been achieved by a generation of regional and local planning.

NATIONAL ECONOMIC POLICY

In a less spectacular way, there have always been environmental implications of regional policies since the Barlow Commission.[8] They include industrial location policies, with their often very detailed control apparatus of industrial development certificates, grants, rebates, premiums, tax concessions, advance factory locations and so on, at a more or less specific level ranging from a whole region (or the province of Ulster) through Special Development Areas down to employment exchange areas and district councils. Whatever one's view of the success or otherwise of these policies, they have involved specific or induced changes in settlement patterns, income levels, the volume of movement, and important impacts on the natural environment, and have indirectly influenced a wide range of private decisions about capital investment.[9] Although regional economic planning councils have been in existence for ten years, their influence on central government thinking has been quite minimal: at best, they have been more or less persuasive advocates of the case for their regions (like the case for a spine road to Plymouth which formed the refrain of every submission from the South West for a decade).[10] It would be difficult to think of a case where the councils have stopped central government from undertaking investment or allocating production, and there are many instances of unsuccessful pleading for jobs, roads or other benefits. Regional policies illustrate, *par excellence,* the nature of the central resource-distributing process. Some twenty years ago, arguments raged as to whether a new integrated steel plant should be located in west central Scotland or South Wales or in Lincolnshire.[11] In the event, eastern South Wales was chosen The venture has not been a success, but it is impossible to say whether this was due to faulty location strategies; certainly unemployment in South Wales is much lower than it was and incomes are higher, but it is not possible to say what relationship this improvement has to the existence of the steel plant.

THE CONTROL OF LOCAL GOVERNMENT

Overriding all other considerations, we need to be clear that the central government has total powers over the operations of local government, not only through the operation of specific legislation and mandatory force of, for instance, the circulars of the Department of the Environment based on that legislation, and through its general power of audit, loan sanction (and surcharge), but also through the whole system of local government finance which is essentially redistributive in character. Recent anxieties about the rising level of local rates have brought home to many people for the first time the uncomfortable fact known to every local finance committee for a long time, that central government subventions, determined by complex formulae over which local authorities exercise no influence, have formed increasing proportions of total revenue spending.[12] In some areas they traditionally account for well over three-quarters of the local budget (e.g. in poor rural fringe districts), and the general average is likely, unless there are drastic changes, to be in excess of the present 60 per cent in the foreseeable future.[13]

The fundamental dilemma is that those local authority

areas which have the higher costs and the most pressing needs also have the lowest revenues and probably a falling tax base.[14] This phenomenon has long been known in the United States, and has given rise to endless arguments about the need for revenue sharing (i.e. an equalisation of burdens between wealthy suburbs and poor city centres), but in the British context this sort of discussion tends to hide the fact of regional inequality – i.e. that all forms of central intervention in local government must be based on the assumption that revenues have to be redistributed from the areas where they are highest to the areas which have the greatest needs (now predominantly Ulster, and to a lesser extent Scotland, Wales and the North). The accident of local boundaries in this connection is generally held to be irrelevant. Thus, London, with a little more than 12 per cent of the population of Britain, generates a quarter of all personal tax revenues; yet the share of incomes accruing to residents overall is very little more than is implied by the national average, and inside the London area these incomes are very badly distributed, so that we have within a few miles of each other the largest concentrations of rateable value and personal and corporate incomes in the country and, on the other hand, boroughs whose tax base is so poor that they should become recipients of government aid on a scale commensurate with that given to some of the poorest and most remote regions. Yet so delicate are the political implications of these redistributive processes that until recently it has been accepted that Scotland was entitled to much bigger benefits in this respect than any English urban area (and the Kilbrandon Commission's statements on the high level of *per capita* infrastructure spending in Scotland are a reflection of this).[15] It is only recently that Scottish nationalism has seen in the taxation of oil revenues a way of ending this dependence – a matter of little comfort to regions which have not had the good fortune to have oil piped ashore on their coastline, or to a London borough which is losing population and employment.

AN APPROACH TO DEVOLUTION

The system we have described clearly depends *de facto* on a high degree of centralised legislation and decision-making. It is accepted that in respect of one essential aspect of the matter, the equality of real incomes, there is no room for fundamental change. Either we believe that within the United Kingdom there should be, as far as possible, equality in living and environmental standards, in which case a central channelling of resources is inevitable, or we think in terms of non-material values (like self-government) assuming such importance that they could one day transcend such mundane matters as real income and levels of service. In a world where nationalism has become more important, we have plenty of examples of countries choosing independence in poverty in preference to colonial dependence, and equally of many countries which have learned to keep their independence to a degree, while maintaining their livelihood through a mixture of compromise, appeal to international aid, and a growing ability to attract private investors. It is not altogether inconceivable, in that sense, that regions might wish to achieve self-determination at the cost of ending the present system of subsidies, but this is not realistic enough to warrant serious consideration (and this much is common to all shades of Kilbrandon opinion).

Perhaps the most extreme illustration of this conflict between a measure of material well-being and other, intangible, benefits, is that of Ulster. The British government has recently made clear the province's degree of economic dependence on the rest of the United Kingdom (other than the cost of maintaining an army and compensation payments).[16] Although, until recently, Ulster had the largest measure of self-government of any part of the United Kingdom, it had at the same time the highest measure of dependence on the rest of the economy. The maintenance of even a fairly low standard of incomes (when compared to the rest of the country) clearly depends on the centralised redistributive function of Whitehall, and for most of the period since the outbreak of large-scale violence in 1969, local self-government has been suspended. Opinions differ as to the environmental effects of British rule with a large armed presence (taking the word in its widest sense), but only very few people believe that Northern Ireland would be a better place to live in without the British army, at least at present, and nobody believes that material standards would be better if the province were independent, or joined up with the Irish Republic.

As the 1974 Discussion Paper showed, environmental expenditure in Northern Ireland in 1973–4 amounted to £142 million, or nearly half the total taxation receipts of the province. Although this sum is not much in excess of UK averages, it illustrates the principle of central allocation and redistribution, apart from the fact that in real terms (e.g. because of the lower unit cost of housing and road construction) it represents a higher rate of creation of assets. Any form of devolution of government (e.g. self-government from Stormont) is dependent, for its functioning, on the allocation, by the London government, of an amount equal to nearly 40 per cent of total expenditure. When we say 'functioning' we mean the maintenance (or achievement) of service standards, including housing, which are perceived as being necessary for the country as a whole. The basis for this conclusion is the impossibility of any other standard. To limit expenditure to what can be raised locally by taxation is to create or maintain indefinitely standards of service much lower than those obtaining elsewhere in the country; to allow the local administration to set the standards would be tantamount to asking the rest of the country to allow themselves to be taxed for purposes over which they have no control.

Naturally this creates what is sometimes called, rather pretentiously, a 'colonial' situation, which is another way of saying that any area or community which cannot within itself produce the revenues necessary to achieve any given standard of performance, must rely on external aid. Under the British system, this largely takes the form of current subventions (and occasionally loans for capital works); the only alternatives are external private sector loans (bonds) or international aid. The first of these alternatives is widely practised by public corporations here, and occasionally by local authorities, in preference to government-arranged loans; and it is the normal way of financing public works in some countries, for instance the United States. External non-repayable aid is sought by many of the newly independent developing countries, but this method too involves ties and conditions of various kinds.

The stress which commentators lay on the client situation which is created by all forms of external help, whether it is perceived by those receiving it or not, helps to underline the nature of the conflict, and disguises the seriousness of the essential nature of the redistributive process, which is that it imposes standards from outside a particular sub-system, and therefore limits the degree of devolution which is possible to something no greater than that now practised in British local government.

The question is therefore, once again: assuming that central government is willing to redistribute income so as to try to maintain or improve the balance of standards between the regions, which types of decision could be reasonably abdicated to regional authorities? The difficulties inherent in the answer turn immediately on the word 'reasonably'. The Kilbrandon Commission, no doubt influenced by the non-government witnesses which came before it, was inclined to dismiss the claim of central government departments that they could do the job more efficiently, as a product of bureaucratic imperialism. They were probably impressed by examples of delays imposed by the need to channel, for instance, planning appeals through London; by the apparently absurd desire for uniformity of standards, and by the insensitivity of the central government to local preferences. Some of their opinions clearly derive straight from Dicey.[17] His jaundiced eye, surveying the legislation being promoted in the early years of this century, saw an electorate determined to 'equalise advantages', and therefore well on the road towards turning what had begun, in Bentham's time, as mere administrative centralism, into progressive collectivism, more and more tinged with socialistic principles, and therefore leading to progressive erosion of individualism, self-reliance and self-determination. Dicey's view of the situation was, as it turns out, perfectly correct; what is surprising is not that a commentator seventy years ago should have recognised the logic of a situation already explicitly accepted by Bentham, but that the Kilbrandon Commissioners should find it worthwhile to perpetuate the myth that an extension of central government powers, functions and financial responsibilities should in some way undermine something not clearly specified but assumed to be part of a great tradition.[18]

But in concentrating, as they did, on the kinds of decisions capable of being devolved on to regional bodies, they fell into the common error of supposing that large decisions can be separated from small ones. In fact, one cannot look at such apparently innocuous matters as the provision of open space for a community, outside a more general framework of land-use policy, the ownership and management of land for public purposes, of regional settlement policy, or transportation strategies. A decision to promote local employment opportunities (such as, for instance, some northern towns pursued before regional policies became general, and perpetuated in those advertisements one occasionally sees, inviting industrialists to take up vacant land in a particular area), is not very meaningful unless it is part of a general investment and fiscal strategy which then allows an entrepreneur to make a genuine choice between locating his plant in Co. Durham, or moving to Cumbria, or staying in Middlesex.

The Strategic Plan for the North West, published in 1974, proposed a programme of cleaning up polluted rivers in the region, according to the degree of urgency. A local or regional authority can take a decision to implement such a policy, but it would do so in a vacuum unless it were assured of the allocation of national funds to finance the programme. Although parallels with events in other countries are often misleading, it is worth pointing out, in this connection, that it is precisely in the field of water management (flood and pollution control) that the United States Federal Government standards are essential to the implementation of any locally conceived plans. Thus (apart from that pioneer example, the Tennessee Valley Authority), the great campaigns which began during the 1960s to clean up America's rivers are managed by state water-pollution control boards which control the activities of local conservancy districts; but financially (and for their powers of enforcement) they depend on federal legislation. Just how important this role can be is shown, for instance, by demands which were put forward by local governments as well as ecological pressure-groups that such federal powers (including heavy daily fines) should be used to force steel companies in Ohio and Indiana to adopt measures to cleanse their effluent, on such a scale as virtually to force their closure, or else to exact subsidies to compensate them for the resultant losses. Similar situations exist in this country, though we are usually careful not to spell them out too clearly. If the river Don is still one of the most polluted in the country, it is not because the old West Riding County Council or its constituent districts were laggard in their attention to environmental standards but because the cost of dealing with the waste products from the South Yorkshire steel industry would have to be borne nationally – since it could not fall either on the local ratepayers, or a steel industry already threatened with bankruptcy. Though the case of pollution is perhaps a somewhat drastic example, the same analysis could be applied to a whole range of environmental problems which cannot be dealt with in isolation. If therefore the Kilbrandon commissioners drew up a list of issues suitable for local determination, it must have been, in many cases, in ignorance of the nature of the problems they listed, as opposed to purely administrative procedures.

They were similarly in error when they discussed different forms of decentralisation. (The fact that the majority of the Commissioners did not in the end support either legislative or executive devolution in England makes no difference to the fundamental fallacies inherent in their categorisation.) In stressing the equalising function of London, in unanimously agreeing that the technological efficiency argument meant continued central control of major investment schemes, and in reserving such matters as 'human rights' to the national parliament,[19] they effectively crippled any possible regional activity.

A moment's reflection will show why this should be so. Effectively, environmental planning depends, as we have seen, on two forms of decision: those relating to development control (essentially negative powers), and those relating to investment decisions (positive powers). Now if, as the Commission thought, it is 'inconceivable that there should be national health services in some regions but not in others'[20] then it is equally logical to say that it is inconceivable that some regions should be permitted to give planning permissions for sub-standard dwellings or industrial plant which harms the environment, in order to speed up the provision of housing and jobs. Most regions would probably consider their historical buildings to be of regional as well as of national interest, but could, say, a nationalist Regional Council be allowed to sanction the development of a supermarket at the expense of a fine Georgian building on the grounds that this was built for a 'foreign' landlord? Should a mining company be given the right to develop in a *national* park because the regional council thinks that jobs are more important than 'foreign' tourists? Unthinkable: Snowdonia or the Cairngorms are *not* local property. And it was after all Whitehall insistence which was responsible for the survival of vernacular materials (or very good imitations) in local building codes. Development control devolution would in practice, then, be confined to what effectively it is now – variations on minor matters of taste.

At this stage it is perhaps worth pointing out that we need to add a third category to the usual simple antithesis between local autonomy and centralised bureaucracy. A simplistic analysis of the development of legislation and administration in the last 150 years propounds, again in the manner of Dicey, the supposed threat to democracy, liberty, individuality and self-reliance which is said to originate from the desire of the London government to meddle in the most minute aspects of daily life at the local level. Devolution is often simply a generic name for the attempt to reverse the progress of centralism, although as we have seen arguments about efficiency figure as frequently as those about less tangible benefits.

But in fact this simple dichotomy does not present a realistic picture of the pressures with which we have to reckon. The essence of the whole environmental movement (a word here taken to mean every form of conservation, preservation, ecological or amenity group) is that it acts independently both of central and local government, and in practice will often oppose one or the other, but most frequently the local authority. Such groups protest and appeal against planning decisions (or sometimes failure to plan) as well as many forms of development or change not under the control of a local planning authority. Equally they will oppose motorways, airports, railway lines, power stations or anything else which they believe to be a threat to the existing or future environment. The fact that social or economic considerations seldom enter into their reasoning differentiates them from elected forms of government. This is not the place to discuss the importance, or the likelihood of the perpetuation, of this form of pressure group, but it comes into our thinking here because inevitably it will throw its weight into the balance against local autonomy, because it will use the right to exercise pressure through the national media, through planning appeals, or through parliamentary debates, to prevent local decisions from being implemented. Unconsciously perhaps, the environmental movement regards the central government, in the manner of Matthew Arnold, as the embodiment of our collective conscience, as opposed to the short-sighted and selfish economic considerations which, or so they suppose, inform the local decision-taking bodies.

The Commission itself understood[21] that the imposition of minimum standards would encourage central government interference, but then proceeded in a general way to indicate that regions, left to themselves, would not deviate too much from nationally acceptable norms. In the end, this belief did not embolden them to put forward proposals based on such trust, but it is worth reflecting that they could not have had it both ways. Either there is *real* devolution, and then one must risk serious departure from the (London) consensus, or devolution becomes a form of release on parole – govern yourselves as long as you do not outrage our national sense of decency. One senses that they must have known this, for in the chapter which asserts that there is scope for devolution,[22] no single function which is now subject to severe control in the environmental field is named as a candidate for regional decisions.

What of the allocation of infrastructure investment? The Kilbrandon Report discussed the idea that each region might be given its 'fair' share of the available national spending programme[23] and then be allowed to distribute this in any way it thought fit. The idea was rejected, but once more it is worth spelling out why this had to be so. First of all, a great many of the investments are integral parts of a national system (e.g. in electricity supply), and these were rightly taken out of the regional budgets at the start of the discussion.[24] Secondly, the Commission was clear about the need for 'demand management'[25] and this in itself involves not only that total investment should not exceed certain limits, but that no sectoral demands (e.g. for capital goods production capacity, skilled labour, etc.) should exceed a feasible share of the total. Unless this were to be achieved by a series of bilateral negotiations, one assumes that the decision needs to be made in London. Without pursuing this argument too far, one concludes that the only decisions of this sort which could be taken regionally would be those which involved no great drain on scarce resources, did not affect, and were not affected by, decisions in other regions, and could not offend national aesthetic or social sensibilities if they went wrong. Such matters would naturally be rather trivial, and they would scarcely justify regional legislative assemblies, or even local semi-autonomous executive bodies. They are regularly referred to the regional planning councils to serve as agenda fodder.[26]

CONSULTATION AND DEVOLUTION – THEORY AND PRACTICE

The Kilbrandon majority, in the end, favoured, for England, a system of regional consultation which has been described as toothless (see the appendix, Scheme F). Potentially, the functions to be assigned to an elected Welsh and Scottish assembly could profoundly affect the way the environment is managed – but in practice, as we have already shown, the scope for deviation from the national norm would be very limited. This is best discussed, not in terms of the rather abstract functional categories, but in terms of concrete sets of decision-making networks.

If there is one region wealthy enough to raise its own running costs, it is the South East, and within that region the GLC area, comprising as it does, even now, over 12 per cent of the national population, might have been thought of as a planning unit capable of making some of its own decisions. Yet it has never been allowed to do so, even where money is not involved, and the Department of the Environment sees to it that no decisions of any importance are determined at the regional or sub-regional level. Thus, matters of dispute about land use continually occur between the GLC and the London boroughs. Pleas have been made (for example, by J. B. Cullingworth[27]) for a metropolitan housing authority to overcome the type of blockage created by these disputes. The Department reserves to itself the right to determine what land, for instance, shall or shall not be used for housing purposes. The justification for this is that where there is, as so often, a straight conflict between local interest (e.g. the preservation of low densities, keeping out inner city populations which may have undesirable characteristics from a suburban point of view) and the regional interest (providing housing for those areas of London which have no room left), a body vulnerable to local pressures like a metropolitan regional housing authority (composed of local authority delegates) would always act in a manner most likely to preserve the *status quo*. The ability of central government to impose new town development corporations can be cited as historical evidence for the assumption that radical land-use changes can only be taken at the centre.

It is instructive, in this context, to read the debates which surrounded the White Paper on Land published in 1974,[28] and the Bill which came before Parliament in 1975, designed to ensure that profits from the development of land accrued to the 'community' rather than to individual landowners. Those who had at one time held high hopes that such legislation would secure housing land for metropolitan authorities unable to perform their strategic housing functions were disappointed with the new legislation. For it once again failed to establish the principle that the allocation of land for essential purposes should be made at the regional level. This could only have been done by either giving powers to the GLC or the metropolitan counties to acquire land inside or outside their areas, if necessary against the wishes of the district (or London Borough) concerned, or by setting up regional land authorities capable of judging what land might be required. As it is there is, as heretofore, only one method by which a local authority can acquire housing land: by applying compulsory purchase powers which have to be granted by the Secretary of State, and against which appeals can be lodged. (This has nothing to do with the fact that once such an order has been granted, the proceeds of the sale may not accrue, as heretofore, to the existing owner, but it has also been shown that the beneficiary is the central exchequer and not the local rate fund.)[29]

Moreover, the delay, inefficiency and remoteness of the present process of government, which formed the starting point of the Kilbrandon Commission's deliberations, are not due to the fact that decision-making processes are centralised instead of being devolved to the regions. They are due to the scarcity of resources, the divergence of aims between government departments, the need for a certain amount of autonomy on the part of national public utility operators, and to the general failure of technical experts to make the reasoning behind their decisions intelligible to a wider public. We have no reason to suppose that these factors would operate differently under a system of regional devolution. Anyone who has watched even a medium-sized local authority at work should know better. Even in a setting where all councillors and officials meet regularly under the same roof, and none live more than a few miles from the population they serve, important decisions are made by secret caucuses, departments work against each other, environmental decisions tend to be matters of disputed prerogatives between a number of committees within the authority, and as likely as not the most important decisions are taken by statutory bodies outside the local authority altogether. Housing land lies idle in one district while another next door needs it urgently; the county will not intervene; the water authority finds it unprofitable to provide main drainage in any case, and so on. Why should anyone suppose things would be better if another level were interposed between the warring departments, councils, and statutory undertakers on one hand, and the central government on the other?

The Kilbrandon Commission rightly considered the experience of other countries, but did not perhaps point out clearly enough that the trends towards centralised decision making are strongest in countries with a federal constitution, in those areas where social problems are most urgent. In the field of urban renewal, for instance, we have recently found that both in the Federal German Republic and the United States of America, the role of the Federal authority is becoming more important over time,[30] precisely because matters of the social peace are involved – community relations, real income distribution, environmental quality. The same applies to regional planning, which involves such matters as transportation investment, industrial location strategies and other infrastructure improvements, even extending to policies with regard to higher education and the arts. In Germany, the degree of financial autonomy of the *Laender* has been seriously questioned in recent years, and the viability of the whole concept is in doubt.[31] In the United States, notwithstanding a degree of independence at local level, a scramble for federal funds is observed whenever a programme is launched, because of the inability of the individual states to make proper provision for a wide variety of services. This is proof enough that autonomy as a principle is willingly sacrificed if compliance with federal standards brings in extra cash.

CONCLUSION

If standards are nationally important, or decision-making involves a call on scarce resources, or projects need funding by an increased national contribution, devolution to the regions is not practicable. If issues can be identified which can safely be left to regional determination, and no additional funds are involved, then their importance is generally not such as to justify the maintenance of a local legislature or executive. If remoteness, insensitivity to local opinion, delays or, most seriously, lack of inter-departmental co-ordination produce decisions which are open to criticism, machinery (or organisational devices) already exist to improve this state of affairs. If this is not being used, because of lack of vigilance or lack of interest, or because there is corruption, or because skilled manpower is lacking, or because the rise of pressure groups with conflicting interests increasingly stultifies any positive forms of government, then the creation of regional authorities cannot provide a remedy.

Such a conclusion is not based on complacency, or any great admiration for the way in which departments of state conduct themselves in particular instances in the environmental field. Nor is it based purely on the poor performance of the existing bodies, since it might justly be claimed that, as they have no work of any significance to perform, they will not attract the efforts of the best talent in each region. Rather is it a reflection of a more general truth, that if a structure works badly, then a mechanistic approach to its reorganisation is not likely to be very fruitful. If, in 1975, public housing is in the doldrums, unemployment is rising, traffic is becoming more congested, blight in old urban areas is spreading and ugly office blocks are being built rather than seemly old buildings being rehabilitated, then one should look at rather more fundamental causes of an evident social malaise than the distribution of decision-making functions between different levels of the governmental hierarchy.

The serious problems of our time are mainly those concerned with economic failure, and with the inadequacy of our distributive system which even in periods of growth leaves some sections of the population seriously disadvantaged, not least in the field of environmental standards. The remedies for these difficulties are unlikely to be found in changes in administrative structure, unless at the same time our notions about the allocation of scarce resources also change. In practice, such progress as has been made, in the last hundred years, towards greater equality of income, wealth and opportunity has owed little to administrative structure as such, except in so far as the functions of local authorities have increasingly been adapted to their role as the agencies of the central government's notions of redistribution, especially in the shape of services which have gradually been extended to larger sections of the population – health, education, welfare, culture and recreation. There is no reason at all why this process should not be improved within the present framework, or any other, provided that two preconditions are fulfilled: that the total product available for allocation does not, at least, become any smaller, and preferably grows again; and secondly, that the remaining gross inequalities are gradually removed by better fiscal and administrative devices. These will depend on a willingness to legislate, not on the scale of the organisations involved.

It is an entirely different matter if we believe that the process of allocation which we call planning would be improved if those affected by it were to be given a greater say in how the environment, for instance, is to be managed. Clearly there is room for change here. But there is no evidence so far that constructive citizen involvement would be greater if decision-making were to be devolved to a regional level, let alone that of a local authority, to a greater extent than now. Indeed, it is much more likely that in the absence of centrally determined standards, local or regional government would deteriorate into factional disputes mainly focused on levels of expenditure, or sectional advantage. Anyone familiar with the history of one of the original organs of local government in this country, the vestry, can see that only the advent of central legislation gradually put an end to corruption, the rule of powerful oligarchies, and the gross mismanagement of our city environment. It was the replacement of enabling acts and voluntary by-laws by central codes, together with the increase in available funds from the centre, which made this form of self-government obsolete.

However, there is considerable scope for increased involvement on the part of individuals and groups in the process of decision making in the environmental field. Until now, the only alternative to apathy and ignorance seems to have been the sectional pressure group, normally formed to oppose a particular project, or to claim more funds for a particular interest. Undoubtedly some improvement is desirable, and it may well be that *ad hoc* organisations may have to be supplemented by permanent neighbourhood councils, or consultative groups at local or regional level. In the field of health service organisation, this sort of representation came into being in 1974, and it remains to be seen how well it will work. However, experiments designed to provide more widespread participation are perfectly feasible, without the creation of new permanent tiers of government at a level far removed from the consciousness of the individual (apart from the impossibility of any real devolution of final decisions, as has been argued previously).

Thus a lack of belief in the possibility, let alone the necessity, of regional government in the field of environmental management is not the product of any complacency about the present process of administration. There is considerable room for improvement, but this is likely to come through a process which has long been familiar in this country and built on foundations laid by the utilitarian ethic. The fact that so much is still unsatisfactory even after all these efforts have been made, is not a reason either for a radical change in the structure such as is implied by devolution, or for the destruction of the system by revolution, but for a careful examination of a process which, although it now requires annually nearly 10 per cent of the gross national product in maintenance and new construction, still leaves us with slums, congestion, pollution and monotony, at least for a substantial minority of the population. This calls for additional efforts, and perhaps new stratagems, but these have not been identified by the Kilbrandon Commission

NOTES AND REFERENCES

1 *Kilbrandon Report*, paras 581–2.
2 Ibid., paras 1190–4.
3 N. Dennis, *People and Planning: the sociology of housing in Sunderland* (Faber, 1970).
J. G. Davies, *The Evangelistic Bureaucrat: a study of a planning exercise in Newcastle-upon-Tyne* (Tavistock Publications, 1972).

4 R. Minns, 'The Significance of Clay Cross: Another Look at District Audit', *Policy and Politics,* 2, no. 4 pp. 309–29.
5 In Appendix D of the Kilbrandon Report, there is a full list of the functions which departments claim to perform.
6 D. McKie, *A Sadly Mismanaged Affair* (Croom Helm, 1973).
7 West Sussex County Council (and the county councils of Berks., Bucks., Herts. and Surrey), *The London area airports and their environment: The future without Maplin* (typescript, June 1974).
8 For a review of changes in regional policies since the time of the Barlow report see D. Eversley, 'Four out-dated assumptions', *Built Environment* (Sep 1974).
9 Second report from the Expenditure Committee, Sessions 1973–4, *Regional Development Incentives,* House of Commons paper, December 1973.
10 *Kilbrandon Report,* paras 205–7, 274.
11 J. Vaizey, *History of British Steel* (Weidenfeld and Nicolson, 1974).
12 *Kilbrandon Report,* paras 661–2.
13 Ibid., para. 661.
14 D. Eversley, 'Old cities, falling populations and rising costs', *Quarterly Bulletin,* GLC Intelligence Unit (Mar 1972).
15 *Kilbrandon Report,* paras 589–91.
16 *Finance and the Economy,* Northern Ireland Discussion Paper (HMSO, 1974).
17 A. V. Dicey, *Law and Public Opinion in England,* 2nd ed. (Macmillan, 1924).
18 Ibid., p. 307.
19 *Kilbrandon Report,* paras 746–55. See also N. Johnson, 'The Royal Commission on the Constitution', *Public Administration* (spring 1974) 1–12.
20 Ibid., para. 709.
21 Ibid., paras 581–5.
22 Ibid., ch. 16.
23 Ibid., paras 562–85.
24 Ibid., para. 698.
25 Ibid., paras 600–4.
26 Ibid., paras 948–9.
27 J. B. Cullingworth, *Report to the Minister of Housing and Local Government on proposals for the transfer of GLC housing to the London boroughs* (MHLG, 1970) vol. 1.
28 Department of the Environment, Scottish Office, Welsh Office, *Land,* Cmnd. 5730 (HMSO, 1974).
29 D. Eversley, 'Land – The Next Steps', *Socialist Commentary* (Dec 1974) 10–12.
30 D. Eversley and R. Psenicka, *Urban renewal in three countries,* OECD (forthcoming).
31 D. Eversley, 'Britain and Germany: local government in perspective', *The Management of Urban Change,* ed. R. Rose (Sage Publications, 1974) pp. 229–67

2 Regional Devolution and the National Health Service

SIR GEORGE GODBER

THE HISTORICAL DEVELOPMENT OF THE REGIONAL COMPONENT

The history of the regional component in health service organisation is important to any consideration of future developments. The Health Service is composed of elements as far apart as the link of the individual family with an individual general medical practice (and the nurses who work with that general practice) and, on the other hand, some services which are provided only at a national, or at least a supra-regional level. There is a continuum which runs through the district, the regional and the national levels into which an area administration has been inserted, more for its links with other services administered at area level, than because it is an essential component in health service organisation. Some of the relationships are necessary administrative elements and some represent only the kind of scientific or professional link that has to exist throughout a service in which the individual practitioners have to communicate with each other at all levels. The link between the periphery and the most highly developed scientific centres existed quite apart from any administrative organisation of the Health Service, and it will continue whatever the administrative background. Before 1948 such links were haphazard, and the use of regional services was certainly incomplete; nor were there resources available for the development of regional services to the level which was required. The introduction of the National Health Service in 1948 was essentially an attempt to generalise the best kind of service, whether peripheral, regional or central.

The first attempt in Britain to generalise about the organisation of health services was contained in the Dawson report, about which many people speak without even having read it.[1] It suggested various levels of health centre development, but the thinking was clearly in terms of curative services based upon various kinds of specialism which would be available in their most highly developed form at regional centres where medical schools existed. Although virtually nothing was done on the basis of the Dawson report, the idea of regionalism persisted and was taken up in some of the earliest health work of the Nuffield Foundation. Regionalisation was an essential component of the organisation of Civil Defence, and health services formed a substantial part of regional responsibility during the war. The idea of regional development was already included in the Ministry of Health's peace-time programme for development of health services, and was carried further in the organisation of the emergency medical services in the year preceding the outbreak of war in 1939. The Nuffield Foundation with its centre of interest on Oxford had already commissioned a regional survey of hospitals for the four counties based on that centre. During the war, in partnership with the Ministry of Health, it also financed surveys of hospital services, undertaken in 1943 and 1944 as a contribution to peacetime reorganisation.[2]

The Civil Defence regionalisation during the war involved most fields of government activity, but in the health field it demonstrated particularly that executive authority at the regional level was needed in order to provide for hospital services and first aid services, not only for air raid casualties, but also for military casualties. The boundaries of regions were quite arbitrarily drawn and were not completely satisfactory for health services. The hospital surveys suggested modifications of these boundaries, for instance in the North West, and the boundaries subsequently drawn for the regionalisation of hospital services were much more rational from the health point of view.

The hospital surveyors in all regions had been unanimous about the need for a regional organisation in order to foster the development of specialist services in medicine. They did not cover services for the mentally ill or handicapped but those, obviously, had to go with the rest. The value of a regional component in health service administration was admirably demonstrated by the major success of the 1950s – the reorganisation of specialist services and the development of what is, in effect, a district specialist service for every centre of a population large enough to need the district general hospital or its equivalent. The essentially local features of community health-care justified their independence from an organisation which was intended to bring about the radical changes needed in the hospital service. The provision of a comprehensive specialist service, region by region, and the development of the Hospital Building Programme which was published in 1962 and has been progressively carried further since, would not have been practicable without a regional system.[3] It is most unlikely that any other form of regional organisation, either co-operative, or the devolution of activities of the Ministry of Health to regions, could have given the same blend of expertise and local knowledge possessed by the Regional Hospital Boards. They may have had many failings but they certainly had many successes; their work has been quite unfairly decried. The advance in the Health Service had made it necessary to undertake reform; that is no reason for being unmindful of what they did achieve.

The administrative system set up by the 1946 Act and introduced with the National Health Service in 1948 was a major step forward, but obviously not a system which would last indefinitely. It was as far as we could reasonably expect to go at the time and a good deal further than a lot of people thought practicable. The changes of April 1974 are equally about as far as we can expect to go at the present time and clearly have their own imperfections.[4] Equally these changes cannot be regarded as a final solution to health service organisation for the indefinite future. The development of health services in this country and in any other is an evolutionary process, and it is not surprising that it has to proceed in this discontinuous manner. In fact, behind occasional major statutory changes there is a continuous process of change both in the content and capacity of the services which are provided for the public and the way in which they are organised locally, regionally and centrally. The same kind of change has occurred in other countries. Sweden, which is the exemplar of good health services, has gone through a similar process of change and its last change led to the development of a regional component, the result very largely of the Swedes' study of the successes of our own.[5] The province of Ontario in Canada had adopted regional arrangements, though not by creating direct administrative responsibility for regional bodies which we found necessary in the last few years. The USSR had as its pattern of organisation a regional component in the Oblast from the very early stages.[6] The People's Republic of China has introduced its own equivalent of the Oblast in its health organisation, and some of the state organisations in the United States have something of the same kind. There must clearly be an intrinsic factor in health care, which makes it necessary to have a regional component in planning and development, if not in administration. Before thinking of the role a regional component should play, it is obviously first necessary to consider what a health service should generally provide.

THE LOCAL DISTRICT AS THE BASIC UNIT

The National Health Service really consists of an infinite number of services given to patients by various health professionals. It is too often simply thought of as the administrative supporting skeleton. No kind of administration is going to be fully successful unless it is viewed in that light. The National Health Service was not divided into three different parts in 1948: a much larger number of separate parts were concentrated into three main components in each district. The change that had become necessary by 1974 was the effective coalescence of those three components in each district. The concept of the Health District is only really seen in 1948 in hospital organisation and that was largely in terms of institutions rather than district service. Yet the reports of the hospital surveyors had repeatedly referred to hospital centres which were natural foci of population, most simply a county town and a rural area round a group of hospitals which could provide the basis for specialised medical service and the recruitment and training of nurses. The closeness of the relationship which ought to exist between specialist and general practice was not then fully appreciated and was obscured by the stresses which resulted from the severance of many general practitioners from their participation in hospital work, for which they might not have the necessary specialist qualifications. As time passed the necessity for the closeness of that relationship became clear and the need for links between hospital and community nursing and between the social services and the hospital were also better appreciated.

By the time the administrative reforms of 1974 were planned, it was clear that the district had to be the basic brick with which the Health Service edifice must be built. That did not mean that a Health Authority must be based on a district, but it did mean that the district was the management unit as well as the professional unit in the sense that the services in a district were interdependent and must be closely linked. This had been greatly reinforced and made more practicable by the development of postgraduate medical education which proceeded so rapidly through the 1960s. The postgraduate institute at the district general hospital became the focal point where the different components of the medical profession could meet and upon which an ongoing eductional programme could be based. Now that these centres are becoming components in multidisciplinary educational centres, their importance is further enhanced. By far the greater part of health care can be provided through a district organisation. Districts are not autonomous in the medical field and often may share staff with other districts, but there must be identifiable unitary development through the district if the health services are to work efficiently. Dentistry fits fairly closely with medicine in this respect and it is beginning to become clear that the nursing relationship is similar.

The district general hospital concept was the first to become clearly established, but it is now being closely followed by the health centre as the point at which community services provided by doctors, nurses, health visitors and midwives are centered. It seems probable that a future development will be the association of dental practice and pharmaceutical and even optical services with the larger health centres at least. In some centres in Scotland, Belfast and in a few health centres in England there have also been specialist consultative sessions and this could be a further development in future. In essence the Health Service will, therefore, be developed within district units each served by a complex of district general hospital- and community-based health centres with the postgraduate centre at the district hospital as the main professional focus. The preventive services are brought into this by the development of the community physician post and the links that the community physician has with those preventive services, mainly environmental, for which the local authority still has responsibility.

In the new administrative set-up the area health authority has the responsibility of organising district management and is the level at which there is an interface with local authority services, education and social welfare especially. The area is the level at which the elective element now comes into administration, partly through the nomination of local-authority elected members to the area health authority. The districts also have their links with local district authorities, through an advisory body (the Community Health Council) together with the sort of officer relationships which will, of course, develop. Since the area authority has planning responsibilities, the question inevitably arises as to whether these will conflict with or make redundant regional planning responsibilities. One must, therefore, consider what is required from a regional level and whether it can be provided in any other way.

THE NECESSARY FUNCTIONS OF THE REGION

Considering the actual clinical services, there are certain specialties which can only derive sufficient work from a population considerably larger than that of any district, and most areas. Such services are required for a relatively small proportion of patients and make heavy demands on scientific backing. They are needed in support of, and often used in consultation with, specialist services, which have to be provided in all districts. For instance, the management of some heart disease, particularly the remedies for some of the congenital heart malformations, can only be provided by specialist cardiological, medical and surgical units which will necessarily serve a population of several millions. There are some forms of surgical treatment which may have to be even more concentrated than this. Much of the treatment of cancer is now by the use of ionising radiations and these are produced by very expensive apparatus which needs to be placed at locations where it can be served by suitably skilled staff and used to the full. A radio-therapy service, therefore, needs to be provided on a regional basis, not only as a means of economy, but also in order to promote efficiency amongst a small number of staff.

There are other clinical specialties of this kind and some of them need to be associated with scientific departments of the universities which are to be found at regional centres. Nevertheless, these regional services are only effective if they operate in a close partnership with the ordinary specialist services required at the district level. The relationship is not unlike that which should exist in the district between general practitioners and specialists. There are certain services which need a regional basis, particularly blood transfusion so that donated blood can be collected and properly processed and made available in the districts to the clinicians who need it. There are other advisory services in, for instance, epidemiology, statistics, toxicology and even biochemistry, in which the consultative arrangements of the university centres may be required. There are some laboratory services, like those for biochemistry, in which expensive, automated apparatus may be required in a smaller number of laboratories than the total of districts, though not necessarily all concentrated at a regional level.

It may be thought that this kind of relationship could be provided by a particular area or district developing services and making them available to others. This is the way in which such development occurred in Sweden, but there, these were university centres which could be supported from the central government which worked closely with them, and a loose arrangement linking the county councils, which were responsible for the district general hospitals, gave sufficient support. That was an arrangement which evolved from a long tradition of group organisation of the county councils in Sweden; something of the kind could conceivably evolve here, but there is no basis for it yet.

Most of the existing regions in Britain have medical schools at their centres. The new Trent region has three medical schools, whereas when it was centred on Sheffield, it had only one; that does not invalidate the point that, generally, the regional centres contain elements which are valuable in support of the district services throughout the region. The universities contribute to another most important component in the development of the health services – the research and educational activities which are stimulated from, if not organised by, the region. Some of those without medical schools such as Lancaster, Reading, Canterbury, Hull, Aston, Brunel and Exeter also do this. Post-graduate education in medicine and dentistry are essential to the future health of the services. There is a well developed partnership, with an executive organisation, in every provincial region now. In London the British Post-Graduate Medical Federation, a department of the University of London, has served the same purpose, working through officers appointed for each of the four metropolitan regions. The relationship in research has not always been as close in all the regions but is well exemplified by the Newcastle region which has always had a research committee linking the teaching hospital with the regional hospitals.

The planning of development of hospital services, though not of community health services, has been a regional exercise and the result of that has been, hitherto, one of the more satisfactory features of the Health Service.[7] Because of the linkage with regional clinical services, it is still necessary to retain a regional overall plan. It would be disastrously wasteful and, further, it would be clinically inefficient, if some of the regional services were developed out of local pride at centres inadequate to support them. The inadequacy would be as much one of the volume of work needed to maintain expertise, as of professional inadequacy. It is, however, in manpower control, particularly in medicine, and to a lesser extent in dentistry, that the region is specially important. The orderly programme of post-graduate training, which should be the basis of the distribution of junior hospital medical staff, can only be provided on a regional basis in accordance with nationally determined standards. It requires interchanges between centres so that doctors, whatever specialty (including general practice) they may intend to enter, can be given adequate experience. In present circumstances it is also an important means of ensuring that the available medical manpower is equitably distributed. Present maldistribution of junior hospital staff and inadequate provision for some of their training is one of the worst features of the hospital service at the present time. A regional organisation is now beginning to correct this, but the process is far from complete.

The importance of the regional tier in securing equitable distribution of funds, as well as resources for capital development, has been manifest. The Hospital Building Programme of 1962 was the product of individual regional plans, and despite the way in which it has been maligned, has been an important factor in health service progress. It would be disastrous to the Health Service if the future physical development of hospital resources was planned without a true regional appreciation of specialist requirements. The individual specialties cannot be treated separately. Their work is related to that of the others and dovetails into them – for instance, neurosurgery and neurology with radiology, or thoracic surgery with clinical physiology, pathology or radiology again. Much of the specialist work in a particular district may be undertaken simply by the staff of that district, but always there is the expectation that in some of their work they will need the support of specialist units operating over a much wider area. The area might sometimes be large enough to carry some of these services but very few of the areas are of that size, and even if they are, the individual highly specialised services need to be related to one another. It is true that in Sweden, for instance, what amounts to a condominium has been used in order to produce the highly specialised services at selected main centres, but in other countries there are many examples of grievous waste and inefficiency, the result of attempting to provide too highly specialised services on too small a basis. For instance in one South American city, I was told that there are twenty-two radioactive cobalt units where probably six would suffice. The result is not only waste, but inefficient use, because work which should be undertaken by people constantly handling problems of this order is dispersed amongst so many that none can have satisfactory experience.

The financial problems are of a different kind. There is wide variation in the local resources available for health, and although it would be possible to produce some levelling up by central grants, as for instance through the Rate Support Grant at present given for local authority services, that has been insufficient in most fields of local authority work hitherto. There is a great advantage in having central financial responsibility, in that there is no need to be constantly considering whether or not a particular patient is entitled to be treated at a particular centre. In the days before the National Health Service there were endless arguments between local authorities about which of them bore the responsibility (and thus the cost) for treating some patients: this applied particularly to Public Assistance. Professional linkages often extend across particular local government boundaries and it would be a cause both of grievance and of inefficiency if those boundaries now were a bar to the free movement of patients.

It is true that most of the district sevices can be managed and substantially planned upon a local pattern, provided that they take account of the overall regional plan. Most of the future services provided outside hospitals are likely to be based upon health centres, and the distant planning of these from a regional centre could have as great disadvantages as the planning of specialised services solely from the district level. The best work in this area has been the result of progressive attitudes in particular authorities able to obtain satisfactory relationships with the professions. That sort of relationship will not be developed by a regional authority which will be remote from much of the region it serves. Some of the best local developments now involve accommodation in a single building, not only for a health centre, but also for the district facilities of the personal social service departments of local authorities. There is therefore every reason for undertaking this kind of planning at the district level on behalf of the area authority. Technical advice in regard to building may be best obtained by arrangements between the area and the region, but the professional health advice required is at the area and distict levels. The environmental work done on behalf of local authorities will be at district level and epidemiological control of communicable disease requires local knowledge which will only exist in the necessary detail there. However, the occasional epidemic incident involving uncommon communicable diseases requires the support of local knowledge by the expertise of individuals conversant with either the clinical or the epidemiological behaviour of that disease. It was recommended by the enquiry into the smallpox incident in London in 1973 that there should be a regional epidemiologist available to advise the local staff even under the then existing circumstances.[8] Because many of the common communicable diseases of past times are now controlled and occur infrequently, the number of doctors with any experience of this kind of work is now small. Again the area authority will not have people who can maintain this kind of expertise (even if they have it now) because they will have too little continuing experience of it. This is a point at which regional consultant help becomes essential. Epidemiological techniques are also required in the study of the effectiveness of a great deal of health service. The amount of expertise available in this area is at present small. Many of the studies will be undertaken by people actually engaged in providing or managing services locally. Few of these will have had much investigative experience, but such work can be undertaken with appropriate guidance from an investigative unit at the regional level. Again some of the largest areas might be able to develop appropriate units themselves, but for a long time to come, and as techniques of investigation are developing, it is likely that the main impetus for this work will come from the regional level, where a close association with a relevant department of the university will be possible. The kind of investigation described by Professor Cochrane into the efficiency of particular clinical methods needs expertise of this kind, and often needs to be carried out in several centres simultaneously making use of the same protocols.[9]

A recent report of the Royal College of Physicians on the management of strokes contained the suggestion that a few demonstration centres might be used for an investigation of the best methods of handling this fairly common condition.[10] Three years ago Sir Keith Joseph, as Secretary of State, suggested that demonstration centres might help us to promote the best methods of developing rehabilitation, or certain geriatric or even psychiatric care. This may seem to be an unfair deployment of services to a few areas, but without such efforts it is unlikely that the best results will be obtained for all areas. Either a regional or a national system of supporting such demonstration centres will be needed.

CENTRAL GUIDANCE AND CONTROL

The district, area and the regional level will all need central guidance and support in certain activities. There have been many examples of national promotion of policies during the first twenty-five years of the Health Service and the better development of national policies was to be one of the features of the reorganisation. Although much of the evolution of health service is the result of local factors, as they are affected by scientific advances in medical science (and to that extent the National Health Service is an organism itself, and worthy of the name 'Leviathan' given to it by Mr Enoch Powell) there have been some striking examples of the effect of national planning in changing the course of events.[11] The Hospital Building Programme has already been mentioned. It was followed by a Health and Welfare Programme produced under the same auspices which stimulated a great deal of the growth in local authority services both in the health and welfare fields.[12] Broad guidelines of this kind will still be required from the central department. Also, manpower control and the development of education in the professional fields will continue to require central guidance even though their peripheral application is a matter for local decision. Any new scientific development, like the discovery of the effect of 1-dopa on Parkinson's Disease, leads automatically to application locally in a way that is not controllable by central or regional edict, even though it may involve, as that advance did, very heavy additional expenditure on the drug bill. There have been other major developments, like services for the treatment of renal failure, which have evolved under central guidance, making use of small expert groups and guiding regional planning, involving even the restriction of unwisely exuberant attempts at development in certain places. Central guidance about the further development of heart transplants nearly two years ago was an excellent example of the way in which the unwise deployment of funds by local areas can be prevented. The evolution of other specialties, for instance that of clinical physiology. would certainly have been much too slow if it had been left simply to local planning. There is an inertia, in the medical profession at least, which inhibits the development of new medical specialties because the older specialists seek to retain control. With science advancing so rapidly in medicine, this can only be disadvantageous. Nevertheless, over-enthusiastic use of, for instance, monitoring apparatus in the management of cardiac infarction could be extremely wasteful and inefficient.

The central influence is not limited only to the rapidly

developing scientific edge of medicine. It is also much concerned with improvement in the organisation of general practice and in the control of new preventive measures. In the other professions, such as nursing, or in the sciences associated with medicine, or in the development of new materials in dentistry, there must also be a central influence if the best use is to be made of new information as it becomes available and if the supply of new equipment is to be organised properly. Britain has the best organised home dialysis service in Europe, mainly because newly developed apparatus was produced in accordance with a bulk order related to a programme of dialysis for the whole country. The development of general practice, and in particular its association with health visitors, home nurses and midwives, was mainly stimulated from the centre, as was the original group practice loans scheme. Health centre development was guided from the centre and urged upon local authorities by the central department. This development will be the main feature in the orderly evolution of health service in future. The Hospital Building Programme, which has already been mentioned, not only had to be financed by a special allocation from the centre, but also had to be developed in an orderly fashion as a result of guidance from the centre based upon an initial investigation into the kind of programme that two of the best organised regions could produce. This central function of collecting information about progress and possible new lines of development of the service and disseminating it, is certainly not less important than the overall central financial control.

The National Health Service has been starved of resources for the last fifteen years and, before that, of capital requirements for the hospital service particularly. There are still great disparities in the local provision in different parts of the country (see the table below). The central influence has been toward levelling up. For example, the health service resources of South Wales before 1948 were, on average, well below those for much of England. There were regions of England that were in some ways nearly as badly served, but the hospital development in South Wales and in North-West Wales was given special priority in the early stages, and the money available to Wales has so far increased that NHS expenditure per head in Wales now exceeds that in England.

The same has not been achieved in England, but the North-East has certainly benefited as compared with some other regions, mainly because of the energy of the regional organisation in the early years.

Undoubtedly more might have been done in England if more resources overall had been available. It has frequently been suggested that the disparities, both geographical and functional, that exist within the Health Service are due to neglect of particular areas. The implication is that a fairer distribution would take something from the areas now relatively well supplied and give it to the others. In fact this sort of intrusion into the pattern is not a practicable method. It implies that what is provided for health services is generally sufficient overall and that the defect is one of maldistribution. The fact is that in England there has been so much smaller provision made than in Scotland, that it has not been possible to provide the extra money that was needed for areas like the North Midlands or the West Midlands, or the North West, where facilities at the inception of the Health Service were nearly as bad in some areas as in South Wales.[13] Because health services develop even locally in an almost organic way, it is really not possible – even if it were desirable – suddenly to cut short what is available in one area and give it elsewhere. If this happens the degree of frustration amongst those concerned would be extreme, and the effect of deprivation on the public served would be such as would certainly bring forth justified and loud protest. It is through the use of additional development money in the right place that one should expect to obtain the kind of levelling up that is required. There is no justification whatsoever for levelling down in England. The method that has been applied successfully to Scotland and to Wales with their independent advocacy for further funds ought to be applied to the areas where there are the greatest defects in England. A regional pattern of government might assist in this.

There are certain medical fields related to the Health Service, more or less, which have to be handled at a national level. The control of safety of drugs is really only practicable through a national system serving the whole UK, and this must be the responsibility of the central department. International contacts in the health field, which are not merely an exercise in the support of developing countries

NATIONAL AND REGIONAL HEALTH EXPENDITURE AND INDICES OF NEED, 1971

Area	*NHS expenditure (£s per capita)*	*Population ('000s)*	*% over 65 years*	*% in social class IV & V*	*Birth rate (per 1000 population)*	*Infant mortality rate* (death of infants under 1 per 1000 live births)
Wales	43.66	2725	13.6	30.6	15.8	16.0
Scotland	50.40	5217	12.3	30.1	16.6	20.0
England	41.87	46,090	13.1	25.9	16.0	17.5
Hospital regions in England:						
S.W. Metropolitan	48.06	3041	14.2	20.1	14.9	15.8
N.W. Metropolitan	46.44	4128	11.7	21.4	16.0	16.9
S.E. Metropolitan	40.22	3547	15.5	24.1	14.3	14.5
N.E. Metropolitan	38.43	3386	12.6	25.2	15.7	16.5
Liverpool	38.36	2217	11.8	31.6	16.9	21.1
South West	36.47	3208	15.6	27.1	15.0	15.6
Leeds	35.28	3240	13.6	28.9	16.4	19.8
Newcastle	34.56	3045	12.6	30.5	16.1	18.9
Manchester	34.48	4582	13.5	27.6	16.4	19.1
Oxford	34.18	2031	11.5	26.6	17.2	15.5
Wessex	33.68	2067	15.2	24.6	15.5	16.4
Birmingham	32.34	5148	11.2	27.0	17.2	17.7
East Anglia	32.01	1790	14.1	31.4	15.9	15.0
Sheffield	30.47	4673	12.2	28.8	16.7	18.8

Sources: Census, 1971; Noyce, Snaith and Trickey[13]; DHSS, Health and Personal Services Statistics.

The national figures are not strictly comparable with the regional figures, as only the former include capital and certain items of central administrative expenditure.

overseas, enable us to ensure an adequate interchange of information with other countries at a comparable stage of development to our own, the establishment of international standards for various drugs and reagents, and the control of certain exchanges, especially now related to communicable disease and probably in future to drugs. We gain at least as much as we give in international exchanges on health. Some of the recent developments in contamination of the environment have made it necessary to develop an expert group in the Department of Health which works with, for instance, the Department of the Environment, the Department of Education and Science, the Ministry of Agriculture, Fisheries and Food, and the Research Councils. Indeed, the central department already collects and disseminates information on this matter, both to the regional and local health authorities, and to others in the professions involved.

DISCUSSION

From what has been said it follows that there are different related activities which must be undertaken at national, regional and local level. The existence, side by side, of English, Scottish, Welsh and Northern Irish Departments is not necessarily a contradiction of this. The other Departments depend to a greater extent than is generally disclosed on the Department in London for certain of the general activities which may be conducted on behalf of all of them, of which international health is only the most obvious, and they are represented in relevant expert bodies. If a comprehensive health service is to be maintained in Britain then that central influence must be maintained also. The question which arises is really the extent to which detailed control should be exercised by the central department over the lower levels. On the more scientific activities the question is fairly straightforward, as the Kilbrandon Commission recognised in relation to research. There is only one body of science, and a dozen different regional interpretations of it would be most inefficient for this or any other country. There need not be precisely similar interpretations of medical science, which indeed the professions would reject, but a uniform approach, for example to immunisation, is needed.

Moreover the trend in other countries, which do not yet possess health services as comprehensively organised as our own, is towards closer integration. The Eastern European countries, of course, for fifty years have had completely integrated services, as has New Zealand. To a large extent the Scandinavian countries, which have the best records in health, also have centrally integrated services under the guidance but not the executive direction of a department. The Netherlands, which has in many ways health records almost as good as Sweden, has a much less organised system but in certain respects, as for instance in the child welfare and maternity services, Sweden does show an advantage over the Netherlands. In Sweden the evolution of the present system has taken place more coherently over a century than in Britain. As a result, more confidence has existed in some of the local organisations, particularly the so-called county councils, than exists in this country. Medicine had been unified at a local level at a much earlier stage than in Britain. The failure to evolve as effective a form of general practice in Sweden as we in Britain have been able to do, probably explains the relatively more costly service provided there (though the Swedes have been prepared to invest more in health, at least within the last fifteen years). It may be relevant that the central agency in Sweden has been the Socialstyrelsen, which is a board of health and welfare with a medical director-general. This board is not the central financial agency, but it has been the guiding agency for many years and originated as the registering authority for doctors over three-hundred years ago.

It is important at this stage to consider future expectations about health care, and the contribution that schemes of regional government can make in meeting them. Despite the debate which goes on in some circles about the possibility of reducing the coverage of the Health Service, it does appear that public expectation is broadly that it should be able to get whatever health care it needs without payment at the time of use. It is increasingly conscious of delays in getting that treatment, but probably unaware of the main factors which produce those delays. Some of these factors are peculiar to the professions concerned, but the strongest overall influence in England and probably in Wales is the general shortage of funds which makes supporting staff too small. The public might accept that it may be necessary for them to contribute more for the use of services, or even to pay more by way of insurance or tax, but it does not seem to think in terms of a less than comprehensive service. General feeling in the professions, apart from the professed wish of some members of the medical and other professions for the opportunity of earning more in private practice, is certainly for making the service more effective and more comprehensive. It hardly seems practicable to think in terms of cutting off this or that piece. For instance, it has been said in at least one political utterance that it was a mistake to provide a dialysis service for renal failure. Renal transplantation will give, for a proportion of patients, a better result than dialysis, but the two are complementary and the one would certainly not develop adequately without the other. It seems most unlikely that the public, or the profession, would accept a situation in which an advance had been made and was not permitted in this country within the Service; it would be impracticable outside it. A black market in dialysis services would not only be invidious, it would be grossly inefficient. It might be possible for us to cut out, for instance, the ophthalmic services, but that would be damaging to the other services concerned with eye diseases and would certainly be a gross disservice to some of the old people for whom we purport to be trying to provide better care. It is too seldom realised that the National Health Service now includes the whole complicated multi-professional structure upon which sound health care depends and peripheral private services function only because they have the National Health Service as a fall-back position.

As has been indicated earlier, we do need a central department to develop, in collaboration with the professions, overall policy objectives. It seems most unlikely that the funds required could be obtained evenly to meet need throughout the country unless they came from central sources. Britain is currently spending only 5.2 per cent of its gross national product on health, compared, say, with 7.4 per cent in Canada and the United States.[14] If England and Wales are to have funds which would produce *per capita* expenditure on the health service equal with Scotland (and there seems no reason why they should have less), then an increase of at least 15–16 per cent is needed. That means additional total expenditure of the order of £400 million a year at present values. Even to bring England up to the rate of expenditure of Wales would mean an addition of some £45 million a year. In a recent table the Office of Health Economics has estimated that an extra £50 million could be raised by 1p on the standard rate of income tax; an increase of 1p a gallon on petrol; an increase of 1p on a packet of twenty cigarettes; a flat rate increase of 4p on the weekly National Insurance stamp; a charge of 40p for each surgery or home visit (assuming 50 per cent would be exempt); an increase of 35p in flat-rate prescription charges (assuming that 50 per cent of patients would be exempt), or a £6 a week charge to offset hotel costs for in-patient care, excluding mental treatment, and assuming that 50 per cent of patients would be exempt.[15] A combination of these various methods might be used, but it is difficult to imagine comparable additions being obtainable through local taxation, unless some kind of local use of income tax was permitted. It is difficult to see how regional institutions could become 'stronger' unless they had a source of finance which they were able to control. That would mean giving the different regions an opportunity of levying taxes of their own in their regions, but it seems difficult to believe that anything approaching the additional £400 million could be obtained by this means to bring England and Wales in line with Scotland. Something might be done, but whether the outcome would be fair to the population as a whole must be doubted.

Anyone familiar with the pattern of development of local authority health services before 1948, despite the fact that they were then limited and at relatively low cost, knows well that the wealth of an authority has a direct bearing on the quality of the service provided. This was not the sole factor, but it was, in my belief, the most important. A county like Surrey, for instance, was able to recruit doctors for its public health services in the 1930s much more easily than a county borough like, say, Bootle, for the simple reason that it offered £600 a year as compared with £500 a year, which was the minimum negotiated rate. Some would see other advantages about living in Surrey rather than on Merseyside. Nevertheless it would be an advantage to have some independence as a result of a different financial contribution. The bulk of the money for the Health Service might still have to come from the centre, but before the recent reorganisation it was certainly easy to see that interested authorities had made extra efforts to provide better sevices. There were areas of the country where child guidance clinics or children's dental services, for instance, had been far better developed than in others. There are wide differences between the proportion of children immunised against various diseases. One does not want to see particular areas in the country go short, but the outcome of stronger regional institutions could be that some areas in the country will show the way by better provision and make it incumbent upon the others to follow.

It seems likely that stronger regional authorities with a little financial autonomy would not merely try to raise money for developments that they themselves thought to be necessary, but would also press for the kind of increase that they should have in their central allocation. The Sheffield hospital region went short throughout the first twenty-five years of the Health Service. This may have been due partly to less forceful officers or members, but it stemmed mainly from the gross deficiency with which that region began and a very rapid increase in population that occurred there. A special effort was made to bring Wales up from behind and that succeeded, but there was no independent political influence used on behalf of the North Midlands. The same arguments might be raised about the West Midlands and the North West generally. In fact, in the Liverpool hospital region, manpower resources were in many ways more generous than in other regions, but the stock of buildings in the hospital service happened to be so bad and the housing situation in the main conurbation also so bad, that the possibility of the region catching up was thereby reduced. At a period when too often the service available was judged by numbers of hospital beds and not by the quality of the work that would be possible in the premises provided, the difficulties of Merseyside may well not have been appreciated. A stronger authority not wholly dependent on the central health department might have made a good deal more noise about this.

It is difficult to envisage any way of strengthening regional authorities without giving them some independent method of obtaining more money. Local health authorities, after allowing for the rate support grant, raised only about 3 per cent of the cost of the National Health Service after the change in personal social services. The most successful regional canvassing for extra funds was by the Scots with the Welsh starting later and a long way behind. That suggests that only separate ministerial advocacy for extra funds from the Exchequer is likely to be effective when the sums involved are so large. A small additional source of revenue at the discretion of the region would be, perhaps rightly, a lever for obtaining more from the centre. Regional authorities past and present had considerable discretion in the way they developed their own services. Some were notably slower and some more active in producing sensible hospital capital development programmes or improving hospital staffing or post-graduate medical education. It may be that the Scottish Home and Health Department with a smaller task and relatively larger staff, as well as its own political regional advocate, was always in a position to exploit whatever opportunity there was within the central financing arrangements. The possibilities of varying priorities according to local wishes within the National Health Service are not very large; they are of emphasis rather than principle, since the use or non-use of say a particular vaccine could hardly be left to local whim without undermining the whole of a prophylactic programme. A regional drive for fluoridation of drinking water would be possible now, as would priority for development of community services over a particular hospital development. Freedom would be most useful in capital work.

Some would argue that stronger regional institutions might cause additional problems. In some respects it is probably true that inefficiency and delay did result from having an extra tier between the department and the district, but that could equally well be due to the intervention of the department in matters of detail, whether through the region, or direct. Much of this stemmed directly from political pressures over points, which, in the earlier days, tended to be referred back to the regions. There was certainly not unnecessary uniformity because the difference between the regions is far greater than it should be. Much of that difference existed in the early days, but the gap has not been closed because additional funds have not been provided and made available to the areas where they were most needed (except in Wales and Scotland).

The new reorganisation provides an administrative frame within which best results can be promoted in such a system. Having listened to my senior medical colleagues in the EEC bewailing the difficulties of developing or maintaining general practice, post-graduate education, or the links between different groups of doctors, I am very well aware of the great advantage we have in having kept such a system of providing primary medical care. We do in fact have a functioning and rational system of providing medical care. All we lack is the fully developed administrative back-up and the money needed to support it: the adequate payment of both professionals and particularly low-paid non-professional staff would be costly, but is essential. There must, in addition, be a large and continuing capital investment, both in the hospital service and in health centres. It was disastrous that the health centre programme, which took so long to develop a real impetus, should have been checked last year before it had reached anything approaching its peak.

Is there scope for devolution of responsibility for health care to local authorities? One particular result of the current reorganisation of the Health Service administration is that there is now provision for a better interface between social welfare and health. It will be argued, of course, that local government should be responsible for health, as well as for the other services. At present local government is not organised on areas which are suitable for this purpose, and the addition that would be necessary to local authority expenditure would be so large that it would require a major fiscal change. In Sweden over 80 per cent of county expenditure is on health. A regional system within local government could hardly be effective unless it had some financial independence. There is certainly a need for greater public involvement in the Health Service, yet there is a real risk that the recent changes rather will produce a reduction It is imperative to make the Community Health Councils work.

The Kilbrandon Report says very little about health but seems to regard it as a subject generally suitable for devolution. There seems to have been no understanding of the nature of the complex links within the service nor of the functional nature of a health region, which has reasons for being the shape and size it is. The need to have a central department which not only deals with the odd collection of functions mentioned in paragraphs 93–5 of Appendix D of the Report, but is also well enough informed about the workings of the National Health Service at regional and district level to be able to reach sensible conclusions on future policy in concert with the professions, does not seem to have been understood. There are examples in other countries of a less direct involvement of the central department in the financial workings of the service – Sweden, Denmark for instance – even though the services are fully organised, but in each case there is a strong professional structure at the centre with considerable authority and a long record of effective guidance.

Besides the functional case, the Kilbrandon Commission was also concerned with bringing the existing regional institutions under direct democratic control. The former organisation of the hospital side of the NHS was not democratic in the sense of being under the control of elected bodies. There was indeed no elected body at the regional level which could have undertaken the urgent task of reorganisation required in 1948. Nor was local government based on units in any way suitable for the development of a hospital and specialist service. The representative element had to be obtained by selection from the people suggested by local authorities to the minister for appointment to Regional Boards and Boards of Governors and to Regional Boards for appointment to Hospital Management Committees. These boards and committees were not responsible to an electorate but they were a great deal more responsive to local feeling than many people suggest. They were certainly subject to attack by any other local body with little chance of reply and they were too often left to be the local whipping-boys for some unpopular decision, such as a closure of a hospital in full accordance with national policy and local service efficiency.

Nevertheless the new organisation is responsible for all the services and has succeeded two classes of authority which were either directly or indirectly elected. The Health Service cannot advance unless there is better co-ordination between community and institutional services. What is done in the community is less technical and more closely associated with other services which are under locally elected control. In the course of a year at least two thirds of the population will use the services and mainly in circumstances of less complete dependence upon the technical elements which must be professionally controlled. It is therefore much more important to ensure that the public locally is able to feel a personal identification with the services it uses and a readiness to respond in them. This brings out an inevitable contrast between management of an intricate complex of interlocking services requiring a small expert group with, on the other hand, liaison requiring a much larger group identifying with the local population but able to keep itself sufficiently informed of people's wants and the pressures under which the professionals trying to meet those wants must work. It is a new kind of exercise such as some other countries have tried to meet in their own way in the past. The main problem is at the district level and in the hands of the Community Health Councils.

The problem at regional level will be more difficult. The regional functions are the most complex technically and the most removed from general public understanding – so much so that it is often difficult to have their necessity understood at all. The technical expertise can be provided through well-planned advisory machinery, which can be better informed and more influential than some small share in membership of the authority itself. Provided the independence of the professional and technical advice is assured and its nature is not capable of suppression, even an elected regional authority might be able to assume the administrative responsibility at regional level. This would be unlikely to succeed unless the natural health regions were used for other purposes, an arrangement that does not seem likely soon if at all. It would be easier and probably functionally more suitable to the special needs of the NHS to use an indirect electoral system which would make possible the inclusion of university and professional nominees. Sweden, Canada, Australia and New Zealand have been able to devise their own *ad hoc* solutions to their comparable problems and for the present time that may well be the best arrangement in Britain if a change is thought necessary. However, it seems most unlikely that the Health Service could sustain further radical change in the next few years without suffering severely.

CONCLUSIONS

A form of regional administration is essential to the proper development and functioning of the National Health Service. Certain highly specialised medical requirements in a health service can only be provided efficently at regional or sub-regional centres which can serve large populations. These highly specialised services however must be planned and developed in a way that is consistent with the planning of the services required in every district. They form part of a complex of services which must be planned regionally. Some require very costly equipment which nonetheless may have a limited service life and should be used intensively through that life. The training of staff for such work must be to nationally devised standards and in numbers which must be controlled nationally. There must be overall control of the use of some manpower – especially doctors – if these graduates trained at great expense are not to be lost or wasted. Control has to be regional in accordance with national plans. This means that the regional level must be able to exercise certain controls over the area or district and itself be subject to national control, not merely guidance.

Regional government which could disregard national control of manpower, levels of remuneration, training and specialty provision could be damaging either because of excess or of parsimony. Boundaries which limited access to particular forms of treatment would be unacceptable to both population and professions.

Decentralisation of administration to regions, which in turn allows the management of local services to be a district function, is essential, but the central departments must play a major part in encouraging the right kind of local development and have sufficient authority to prevent a development which is wholly at variance with the scientific evidence. This is not a matter of detailed guidance on many aspects but of defining the optimal pattern of advances which are generally applicable. It should not inhibit, for example, variations in health centre design but it should be explicit in questions involving general medical scientific principles such as the use of a new vaccine or the development of new facilities for a recently defined form of cancer therapy. This does not mean clinical direction but only the provision of an opportunity to use a single system where that has advantages.

A great difficulty would surround the division of responsibility between the central department and the regions in any scheme of devolution. Scotland and Wales already have some responsibility and their population is almost within the range of the English regions. Even they join in central activities with the Department of Health and Social Security, Wales more than Scotland. The main negotiations with doctors and dentists and the salary negotiations are jointly undertaken and this could hardly change. The National Health Service moves forward in some measure as the result of the continued scientific advance which is only possible in general application if administrative provision is made for it. Many changes are simply modifications which the individual doctor makes without outside intervention, but major changes often require development of laboratory or other facilities. Much equipment has been made available on a national scale within the resources available only because of central action. In Sweden a consortium had to be provided to do this. As medicine and its related sciences and professions become ever more complex some sort of national overall programme becomes essential. Education and training for the professions, including health service administrators, also must be nationally planned and provided on a supra-regional basis. Even some clinical or scientific services must be provided at one or a few places for the whole country, presenting problems of organisation and of finance. There would be great loss in effectiveness if the means of central promotion and sometimes restraint were removed.

On the other hand the example of Scotland in securing a large and increasing advantage in funds and manpower and the more recent relative gain by Wales shows how the urgent needs of other regions, which have no separate line of approach to central funds, can fail to obtain recognition. The advantages accruing to Scotland and Wales in the past, because of their special positions and administration arrangements, are important in the debate about regional devolution, not only in respect of the health service, but also with respect to how we organise our system of government as a whole. Moreover, the quality of services, both health and otherwise, might be improved by the creation of stronger regional institutions, as the progressive authorities may set an example which others may feel they must follow.

NOTES AND REFERENCES

1 Ministry of Health, *Future Provision of Medical and Allied Services*, interim report of the Consultative Council on Medical and Allied Services, Cmnd. 693 (HMSO, 1920).
2 Ministry of Health, *Hospital Surveys*, 7 regional volumes (HMSO, 1945).
3 Ministry of Health, *Hospital Plan for England and Wales*, Cmnd. 1604 (HMSO, 1962).
4 See National Health Service Reorganisation Act, 1973.
5 A. Engel, *Perspectives in Health Planning* (Athlone Press, 1968).
6 I. Douglas-Wilson and G. McLauchlan (eds), *Health Service Prospects* (Nuffield Provincial Hospitals Trust and *The Lancet*, 1973).
7 J. Revans and G. McLauchlan, *Postgraduate Medical Education* (Nuffield Provincial Hospitals Trust, 1967).
8 Department of Health and Social Security, *Report of the Committee of Inquiry into the Smallpox Outbreak in London in March and April 1973*, Cmnd. 5626 (HMSO, 1973).
9 A. L. Cochrane, *Effectiveness and Efficiency* (Nuffield Provincial Hospitals Trust, 1972).
10 Royal College of Physicians of London, *Report of Working Group on Strokes* (July, 1974).
11 J. E. Powell, 'Lumbering Leviathan', *British Medical Journal*, II (5 Nov. 1960) 1369.
12 Ministry of Health, *Health and Welfare: The Development of Community Care*, Cmnd. 1973 (HMSO, 1963).
13 J. Noyce, A. H. Snaith and A. J. Trickey, 'Regional Variations in Financial Allocations', *The Lancet*, I (30 Mar 1974) 554.
14 R. Maxwell, *Health Care: the Growing Dilemma* (McKinsey and Co., 1974).
15 M. C. Hardie, 'What Should we Spend on Health Care', *Long Range Planning*, 7, 1 (Feb 1974) 2–9.

3 Regional Devolution and Education

TIMOTHY RAISON

My task is to examine what gains and losses might result from a reorganisation of education in England on the lines set out in the Kilbrandon Report; but one or two preliminary generalisations may be worth making.

For a start, I doubt whether it is realistic to think of any further major reorganisation affecting local government and health in England for some time to come. They have just been through such reorganisations; and the need to consolidate is desperate. And while in theory Kilbrandon is concerned with devolution of power from the centre to the regions, rather than with transfer of power to the regions from local authorities, in reality the fracturing of the present local-national link would be bound to create disturbance. I believe also – though it is hard to prove with figures – that further reorganisation would be expensive. Reorganisation *always* seems expensive, and not only in the short term; and I would be profoundly sceptical about any claim that it is possible to add an additional tier without spending appreciably more money. Kilbrandon does not adequately face up to this; but in the sort of economic climate which we now inhabit it must be a significant factor. English regionalism seems to me therefore anyway something that would have to wait. But there are other objections.

One is whether there is sufficient regional consciousness in England on which to base regional government. It is interesting that only one per cent of those interviewed in England in the Kilbrandon attitudes survey spontaneously suggested regional self-determination as a way of improving things in their area (as against 20 per cent in Scotland and 9 per cent in Wales).[1] I doubt myself whether it makes sense to base units of government on areas which have no real sense of identity; and while I recognise that the South West, North West or North East may be much nearer to such a sense than the South East, I am not persuaded that it is anywhere near strong enough overall to justify a regional tier.

If Kilbrandon does not persuade me on this point, it is very much more feeble on the other side of the coin – the likely effectiveness of services under a regional government. I shall return to this point in more detail, and only say here that Kilbrandon seems to me too concerned with rather hazily articulated (or discovered) attitudes; and too little with the actual implications and consequences of their proposals.

I also question whether the insertion of a regional tier will in fact make people feel closer to decisions. It may indeed make power seem further away – the region could seem to be a barrier between the top and the bottom. I doubt if the introduction of a regional tier in the Prison Service has made prison officers feel closer to power. Moreover, experience suggests that the member of parliament is for many people a more real presence than their local councillor. Is there any reason to assume that a regional elected representative would seem closer than an MP? In fact – to take the nearest analogy we have – I suspect that a GLC councillor is more remote than either an MP or a London borough councillor. At the same time, what can we expect of the mass media, through which regional government and its leaders would have to be projected if it was to involve people? Regional television is there, though it would need considerable adaptation to fit likely regional boundaries. But a regional (as opposed to local) press is largely non-existent. Perhaps coverage would evolve; but this question should have been considered by Kilbrandon.

One other general point seems worth discussing here. It is held by some regionalists that to look at the issue of regional government service by service and to analyse each separately, is to miss the point of regionalism – which is the effective allocation of total resources within the region.

There may be something in this, if one believes that the regional unit is in fact appropriate for all services. But if one does not, then this argument weakens what seems to me one conceivably tenable approach to English regionalism: a decision to allocate to a regional authority only those services for which the region seems the right administrative unit. In other words, the case for a regional tier must be more persuasive if its advocates said that it would cover, say, health and water, and possibly one or two other services, such as police and some form of economic and physical planning, but would not be concerned with personal social services, education, housing and so on, all of which are better left to local authorities. A clear-cut allocation of services to particular levels of government seems preferable to the sorts of division between strategic and tactical, or planning and executive, which are inherent in the Kilbrandon-type approach. We already see difficulties in local government over such divided or delegated matters as planning, transport and sometimes housing, and I doubt whether experience suggests that division or delegation are in principle desirable. Clearly, however, if the responsibility for services were allocated in this way, there would have to be effective arrangements for co-operation between, say, health and the social services – but that problem already exists.

In the survey which follows, I put the emphasis on higher and further education, because it is there that the arguments for regionalism seem strongest. I try to present a picture of what regionalism in education at present comprises, and then to discuss the arguments for increasing it. What I find difficult to do is to analyse the educational implications of the argument which I have just mentioned – that regional government would make for a better allocation of available resources between different services, so that in one region housing would get more; in another, education, and so on. This argument assumes that national government is too remote or insensitive to determine this, but that local governments are too small in their scope for this purpose.

Obviously there has to be a mechanism for the allocation of resources, and no doubt there are flaws in the way this is done at both national and local level. But the advocates of regionalism surely ought to argue in more detail than they have done exactly what resource allocations are not being adequately made under the present set-up, but would be more adequately made under new arrangements. Are there cases of colleges of further education or schools being sited without due regard for physical or economic planning developments? And if there are, was the failure due to local authority, national government or both? These questions are very well worth raising; but in the absence of substantial evidence of such failure it is difficult to assess whether a regional tier would have coped better. Let me now turn to the present position.

THE DEVELOPMENT OF A REGIONAL COMPONENT

Section I of the 1944 Education Act, as revised, reads:

> It shall be the duty of the Secretary of State for Education and Science to promote the education of the people of England and Wales and the progressive development of institutions devoted to that purpose, and to secure the effective execution by local authorities, under his control and direction, of the national policy for providing a varied and comprehensive education service in every area.

In fact the Secretary of State for Wales now has responsibility for the the Welsh schools, but this paper is concerned only with the English system. This pattern of a national system, locally administered, includes very little administration or activity on a regional basis. True, the country is divided up into regions or divisions by the Department of Education and Science (DES), and HM Inspectorate is organised regionally. But only in further education does regionalism cover any institution which is more than a decentralised unit of the DES.

The universities (which, of course, are not regulated by the 1944 Act) deal with the University Grants Committee (UGC), and the DES, at national level. There are no formal regional bodies set up between universities although there are some informal arrangements for buying things like computers. But these arrangements are not in their essence regional. Nor, of course, is there at present a policy of requiring or even encouraging students to attend universities in their own locality.

When we come to other forms of higher education and further education it becomes possible to see rather greater indications of regionalism. Perhaps it should be made clear first that statutorily there is no real concept of higher education: the Education Acts recognise only a system of Further Education. The Secretary of State has the same general responsibility for FE institutions that he has for schools; and these institutions are almost all maintained or assisted by local authorities. They may provide advanced or non-advanced courses, or both. The phrase higher education is normally used to cover advanced courses; as such it may therefore embrace universities as well as local authority institutions. But one cannot say that there is a higher education sector. This would only be possible if there were a sharp distinction between advanced and non-advanced course colleges.

Nevertheless, the Further Education regulations of 1969 recognise the distinction between advanced or higher and other FE work, in that the provision of any course at advanced level requires the Secretary of State's approval. According to the evidence given by the DES to the Commons Expenditure Committee's Education and Arts sub-committee, 'Responsibility for dealing with proposals to provide advanced courses is devolved upon the Regional Staff Inspectors who work in close consultation with their specialist colleagues and consider proposals in the light of the recommendations made about them by the appropriate Regional Advisory Council for Further Education.'[2] Between them, the inspectors and the nine English Regional Advisory Councils (RAC's), which also advise on non-advanced work, constitute an embryonic regionalism which does not exist elsewhere in the English educational system. The RAC's do not exactly match the DES's eight English regional divisions, in that the Northern Division has two RACs, while the North Midland and Midland divisions are matched by East Midlands and West Midlands RACs.

When we turn to school education, we can see almost nothing regional at present (except in Wales and Scotland). The DES has its regional inspectors based on eight regional offices, who are matched by eight middle-grade civil servants (Principals) at DES headquarters with responsibility for regional groups of local authorities. Local authorities also occasionally collaborate on such things as building systems like CLASP and MACE. But overwhelmingly the school system is run by the LEAs and the DES. There is perhaps one point where the region assumes a limited significance – the school (and further education) building programme. Here the allocation is made by the appropriate Assistant Secretary to the territorial Principals in charge of regions and takes regional needs into account. The Principals, with the aid of HMIs, then propose an allocation of the money within their territory. But this process (described by Griffith) is no more than administrative delegation within the DES.[3]

Why is it that the English educational system betrays so little sign of regionalism? The initial answer is, of course, history. The universities began with the ancient foundations of Oxford and Cambridge. Durham was created on roughly the same model by an Act of Parliament of 1832. The growth of London University was more complicated; but it was seen essentially as the university of the capital city, rather than as in any sense a regional institution The nearest the universities have come to a regional entity was perhaps through the Victoria University which, in its prime, embraced a federation of colleges in Yorkshire and Lancashire, and which spawned the present universities of Manchester, Leeds and Liverpool. Durham and Newcastle also constituted a federal university, as did the University of Wales.

These federal universities were all based on geographical areas; and the two English ones anyway had a strong sense (which can perhaps be associated with regionalism) of the importance of serving the economic needs of their part of the world. But it is difficult to argue that their organisation was regional in any form recognisable to Kilbrandon and the creation of the University Grants Committee in 1919 was, in a sense, a formal recognition that universities were national rather than regional institutions. The more recent universities have conformed to this pattern, though, naturally, decisions about their siting have been taken with a clear view of the needs of, and opportunities in, different parts of the country.

In further education, as I have said, hints of regionalism are more evident. One of the forerunners of the modern system of FE were the schools of design. The first was set up with the aid of a government grant in London in 1836. Then between 1841 and 1852, seventeen provincial schools of design were launched, again with government backing. Later on in the century, concern about our technical education intensified, and a number of major developments followed; but again what happened can only be said to be regional in the sense that the new institutions were spread across the country, with an eye to the needs of local industry. The present pattern of control of technical or FE colleges was largely laid down by the 1902 Education Act, which created the local education authorities. The gradual evolution of preponderantly higher-based institutions to colleges of advanced technology and then universities was again regional in the sense that the important decisions were taken with a view to an effective spread of the institutions across the country – certain colleges were indeed designated as Regional Colleges – but not as part of any philosophy of an England consciously divided into administrative regions.

When it comes to the schools, one can only say that the administrative basis since 1902 has been the local education authority (LEA) dealing with the national government. The history of the British school system is tangled, to put it mildly; but essentially the story is one of local initiatives sometimes spurred on or regulated by national concern for educational standards. Outside London, the county, the now extinct county borough and the new metropolitan district have served as the unit of organisation. Certainly, these have at times seemed too small for the job – and recognition of this was one of the motives behind the Local Government Act of 1972, which substantially reduced the number of education authorities. Except perhaps in the West Riding (where a large authority was broken up), there has not been much sign of dissatisfaction with the size of the new authorities. In London, whose local government structure was reformed a decade earlier, one hears it said that some of the outer boroughs are too small – but conversely that the Inner London Education Authority is too big. But overall, pressure for regional-scale authorities to run our schools is hard to find.

Clearly, then, our education system has evolved, from the first, in a world in which regional considerations have played little part – unless by regional considerations we merely mean a belief that we should strengthen our education in all parts of the country. However, over the last decade or so, two official reports on our structure of government have recommended changes in this historical trend: the Redcliffe-Maud Report on Local Government,[4] and the Kilbrandon Report itself.

The former is a much less radical document than the latter, as it argues that provincial councils, at regional level, might take on only a slightly strengthened role in the planning of higher education. These provincial councils in England 'will be well placed to assess provincial priorities in further education, and to settle which existing centres should be expanded and where new ones should be placed'.[5] They would act in consultation with the main authorities and the universities; and seek the advice of the DES on individual proposals and generally act in accordance with DES policies. 'The provincial council should not, however, assume operational responsibility for further education . . . No gain outweighing the disadvantages of divided responsibility would result from giving this part of the service to provincial councils'.[6] Otherwise, provincial councils would apparently play a role in these matters which call for co-operation between main authorities, and would specifically exercise a broad planning function in the specialist education of handicapped and other children where provision in a limited number of centres will meet the needs of the provinces as a whole.

The Kilbrandon Report had a number of things to say about strengthening the regional component in education, but, in assessing these, one runs into difficulties due to the way in which Kilbrandon approached the task. For Kilbrandon is relatively unspecific about services and their efficiency: it is much more concerned about attitudes. One could sum this up by saying that its essence is distilled in the conclusion that 'Devolution could do much to reduce discontent with the system of government. It would counter over-centralisation and, to a lesser extent, strengthen democracy; in Scotland and Wales it would be a response to national feeling'.[7] Having taken this view, in effect the report then goes on to translate the need for devolution into regional structures; but it does not really set out to show whether the regional set-up would in each case work 'better' than the present set-up does, even by Kilbrandon's own yardsticks.

At one point, it is suggested that with environmental, education, health and social services there is considerable scope for devolution of functions of the kind which have been transferred to the Scottish and Welsh Offices. 'They are all, to a greater or lesser extent, capable of being administered in distinctive regional styles; and if policies diverged there would on all sides be a strong incentive, if only on grounds of self-interest, to ensure that differences were kept within the bounds of acceptability'.[8] This question of the level of acceptable variation is of course a recurring theme in Kilbrandon.

The next significant section for education comes in Chapter 18 on executive devolution. The Report describes some of the Secretary of State's present powers, and says that there would have to be an apportionment of them between central and regional government.

> Central policy would have to be prescribed in such detail as to preclude what would be regarded as excessive regional variations. On the one hand there would be what some would regard as a welcome check on the power of the central government, which would be required to lay down its policies more openly and with greater precision than at present and would have less scope for government by administrative decision. On the other hand some of the valuable flexibility which the existing statute allows would be lost.[9]

Later, the Report talks of the specific power which might be transferred from the centre to the regions.

> In education, for example, they might be responsible for the general supervision of local education authorities, including the inspection of schools, for the grant of all approvals of development plans and of schemes of provision for primary, secondary, special and further education and for the control of capital investment.[10]

Appendix D of the Report then goes on to discuss the scope for devolution of DES functions to the region. It is worth looking at these paragraphs in full, but in essence their conclusions are as follows:

1 *Schools*: devolution possible. If *policy* were devolved, there could be problems for children moving from one region to another. Policy could remain at centre, with only *execution* devolved.
2 *Further Education*: devolution possible, but co-ordination required between regions to avoid unnecessary duplication.

3 *Teacher-training*: if run regionally, problems could arise of matching supply to demand and of distribution. Joint action on training and qualifications would probably be necessary.
4 *Universities*: formidable obstacles in replacing a British university system by a number of other systems. Responsibility for student awards could be devolved, but regions might find it desirable to seek agreement on rates of award.
5 *Non-vocational adult education and the youth service*: devolution possible.
6 *Arts, museums, libraries*: could be devolved. Special arrangements might be needed for the support of institutions of more than regional significance.

The Memorandum of Dissent probes the educational implications of devolution rather more deeply than does the main report. Their five English assemblies and governments would plan physical, social and economic development within their areas and have general competence to act for the welfare and good of the people in their area. They would decide the right balance of functional spending as between roads, hospitals, schools, housing, water, etc. They would run primary and secondary schools, nursery schools, and further education in the way that the Scottish and Welsh Offices already do. However, they would do this within the framework of the UK legislation: for example, the UK government might lay down that all state school education should be on comprehensive lines, but the region should decide the exact form. HMI's would remain national, but their reports would also go to the regional government.

The educational responsibilities of local authorities would remain substantially unaltered; but in most cases they would deal with the region rather than the DES. This, it is claimed, would give them very considerable advantages. Decision would be taken by people closer to the local authorities; the local authorities would have representatives on the regional education committees, and the balance of power between the local authorities and the tier above would be more even. 'Local authorities, then, could well gain substantially from the removal of the now powerful, remote, insensitive hand of Whitehall'.[11] Appendix C to the Memorandum of Dissent gives considerable details on the distribution of education (and housing) functions under the Hunt-Peacock scheme of executive devolution. I will not attempt to summarise it though I return to it later; but it is extremely specific in a way that the main Kilbrandon report never seeks to be.

THE POSSIBILITIES FOR REGIONAL ORGANISATION

At this point, I want to set out in a little more detail some of the factors governing possible regional organisation in each of the three sectors of education. It may be argued that it is the essence of the regional approach that the distinction between the three sectors should disappear, or be substantially modified. In particular, there is a school of thought which favours bringing together all higher work – university and non-university – as one sector. It is also argued that there should be a single sector for 16 to 19 year-olds, which again could be organised on a regional basis. I shall come to these views when I discuss the pros and cons of educational regionalism later on in this chapter. Here, for convenience of analysis I shall stick to the threefold system.

Let me start with the universities. The Kilbrandon Commission briefly considered the question of whether the universities might be regionalised; but came up with the view that

> Although the universities have links with other institutions of education and there might on this account be something to be said for giving responsibility for them to the bodies responsible for others forms of education, there would be formidable obstacles in the way of replacing a British university system by a number of regional systems. Responsibility for student awards might be devolved, but regions might find it desirable to seek agreement on rates of award.[12]

In coming to this view, it would be surprising if the Commission were not strongly influenced by the memorandum submitted by the Committee of Vice-Chancellors and Principals of the Universities of the United Kingdom. Part of their evidence was as follows:

> We think the consequences of any division of the university community would be generally damaging to its inter-

> national standing and to the contribution which it makes to the country's welfare. If the British universities are to retain their present character and maintain their international reputation for high standards of scholarship, it is vital that nothing should be done which might inhibit the flow of men and ideas between them or indeed prevent them from continuing to recruit students from the United Kingdom as a whole. We regard it as essential to the nature of the university system that the broad strategy and the allocation of resources should be determined on a United Kingdom basis. In our opinion, therefore, the most appropriate arrangement is for the financing of the universities to continue to be centrally considered and co-ordinated through the University Grants Committee. Similar considerations apply to the relations between the universities and the research councils, where again any failure to consider the universities on a U.K. basis would make impossible the rational allocation of resources for research in the universities. This view, already established in 'big science' will increasingly come to apply to other fields of research in science, medicine and social science.[13]

The arguments presented here are important. The United Kingdom is not so vast a country as to make a certain intimacy between institutions like universities impossible; and there is no reason to believe that universities would gain by replacing the relatively non-bureaucratic UGC system by an inevitably more bureaucratic regional set-up. Moreover, as Kilbrandon presumably felt, decisions of the 'big-science' type have got to be national; while the Commission's comments on student awards are frankly feeble. The basis of the awards is bound to be nationally negotiated. The discretionary element and the administration of awards are at present local authority concerns; to put them on to the regions would be contrary to the Kilbrandon philosophy of devolution downwards from central government, rather than upwards from local government.

There is, however, another point of view which, it is fair to say, is rooted in objections to the 'binary' system of higher education – the system by which university and other higher education are run on separate but parallel lines. This view sees the binary notion as élitist, leading to unequal treatment of the two sectors, and believes that all higher education should be brought under one umbrella. It does not follow that this umbrella should be at regional level: some argue, as we shall see, that the need is for a national higher education commission. But there is clearly a case for saying that either such a national organisation should be sub-divided on a regional basis; or that it should be allocated to regional governments.

The Commons Expenditure Committee in its report on Further and Higher Education (Session 1972–3) followed the earlier Select Committee on Education's view that there should be a Higher Education Commission 'to have overall responsibility for advising the Minister on the administration and financing of the whole higher education sector, and for its planning and coordination'.[14] In other words, it wanted to do away with the binary system. The new commission would apparently, *inter alia,* take over the functions of the UGC and the Council for National Academic Awards.

This system would be primarily a national system. The committee felt however the need for some regional element. They discuss the actual and potential role of the Regional Advisory Councils. They say that 'A national planning body such as we have suggested would however be unable to operate effectively without properly constituted machinery for providing regular information about the requirements of the various regions.' The RACs could do this. At present, there are nine RACs in England. Evidence submitted by the DES to the Expenditure Committee summarises their functions as

> advising on and co-ordinating the development of FE in the region, assessing the needs of industry and commerce and advising LEAs on the provision of the necessary courses, facilitating the dissemination of information on FE opportunities in the region, and encouraging the training of further education teachers. . . . RACs have the function of making recommendations to the Department on proposals for new courses which require the Secretary of State's approval.[15]

As the Expenditure Committee pointed out, the RACs want to play a positive role in planning but feel themselves inhibited by various factors.

> They form an essential part of the machinery for the approval of new courses, but at the same time they have no direct access to information about the future building programme, which is agreed independently between DES and the individual LEAs. Moreover, though university representatives sit on RACs, this is apparently a 'one-way relationship'; having no official channels of communication with the universities, they learn only incidentally about planning in that sector.[16]

The Expenditure Committee argued that the RACs should advise the proposed Higher Education Commission on the provision of advanced courses, while also acting as a link between the non-advanced, local authority sector and all HE institutions within the region, as well as providing a regional source of information for both the national Manpower Council (proposed by the Expenditure Committee) and the HE Commission. Universities should be represented on RACs and 'formal machinery should be established to ensure co-ordination both between neighbouring RACs and with Economic Planning Councils'.[17] The areas covered by the RACs and planning councils should be co-terminous.

Since the Expenditure Committee reported, there has been one development of some potential significance from a regional point of view in the non-university higher education sector. This relates to teacher training. The 1972 white paper, *Education: A Framework for Expansion,* say 'Regional responsibility for the co-ordination and supervision of teacher training has, since the war, rested without major change with 20 Area Training Organisations (ATOs), on which universities, colleges of education, local authorities and teaching professions are represented'.[18]

The James report, *Teacher Education and Training,* which came out earlier in 1972,[19] advocated the creation of Regional Councils for Colleges and Departments of Education (RCCDEs). Each RCCDE was to represent and bring into partnership all the colleges, universities, polytechnics and LEAs in the region. There were to be fifteen regions, of which Wales should be one and the Inner London Education Authority area another. Above this structure there would be a National Council for Teaching, Education and Training (NCTET).

A typical RCCDE would contain about two or three universities and one or two polytechnics, together with about ten colleges. Each would have a governing council drawn from the colleges, universities and polytechnics, LEA's and teachers from schools and FE. There would also be a representative from the Council for National Academic Awards and another from the Open University, and two members nominated by the Secretary of State. The role of the RCCDE's is set out in the James Report:

> Acting within the guidelines provided by the NCTET, the RCCDE's would be responsible for planning the total provision within their regions. They would have to ensure that the size and composition of their student population accorded with the national indicators and would have to make recommendations, in consultation with LEA's and other providing bodies, on the development of individual colleges and on the distribution of first, second and third cycle places, together with the number and location of any places leading to the award of degrees other than the BA (Ed.). As an essential part of this planning process, the RCCDE's would seek a proper degree of rationalisation in the courses offered by their institutions. . . . The whole planning process would require a continuing dialogue between the central body and the regions. The Director of each RCCDE would be a key figure: he would be employed by the RCCDE, above all, for his administrative skill as an educational planner, and he would need a staff which would have to be of good quality. The administrative costs of running the RCCDE and the NCTET should be met by direct grant from DES.[20]

The 1972 white paper accepted the view of the James' Committee that new regional machinery is required. The government therefore proposed that, after further consultation, the Secretary of State should establish, in place of the existing university-based ATO's, new regional committees to co-ordinate the education and training of teachers, composed in such a way as properly to reflect these three sets of interests. These committees would not have executive or financial responsibility for the services they co-ordinated; this would remain with the local education authorities and the training agencies who will need to include in their estimates suitable provision for in-service training. The administrative costs of the committee would be met by direct grant from the Department. The new policy for the Colleges of Education has, of course, the effect of making it increasingly difficult to separate the control and co-ordination of the provision of courses of teacher education from that of other advanced courses. The present government is aware of this, and, while continuing discussions, has devised some interim arrangements.[21]

In all this, one can see emerging some sort of regional planning machinery for non-university higher education – though administration is firmly left with the local authorities. The next step could be a decision to merge the regional co-ordinating machinery for teacher training and the other colleges. Whether this will actually happen would presumably depend on whether the notion of separate education for potential teachers is radically altered.

If some sort of overall co-ordinating machine does develop on these lines, would it be best run by an elected regional government? At present the RACs are essentially co-operative bodies. They clearly feel rather powerless, and there seems to be a good case for strengthening them. There is also a good case for saying that the regional advisory bodies should cover the same territories as the regional economic and physical planning bodies. There are clearly significant planning and economic factors in the siting and developing of FE colleges, and common catchment areas could assist joint discussion. The question is whether co-operation (under the eye of the DES) is sufficient; or whether effective planning can be only achieved by the introduction of a Kilbrandon-type additional tier of government.

Finally, the schools. As I have said already, the school system developed in a non-regional world, with a degree of administrative regional subdivision within the DES representing effectively the only exception. Since the Kilbrandon Report itself was rather skimpy on the whole topic of educational devolution, it seems more sensible to turn to the Memorandum of Dissent for an idea of what education powers might be conferred on their intermediate level of government.

Appendix C sets out the educational functions which might go to intermediate level government (embracing FE as well as schools functions):

a) drawing up, in consultation with the local authorities a five-year educational development plan covering the area's needs for primary, secondary and further education. The plans would include estimates of current and capital costs. They would be up-dated each year. Naturally the whole operation would involve discussions with the Department of Education to whom the general proposals would be eventually submitted.

b) general supervision of the local education authorities in their area to ensure that they are efficiently fulfilling both their responsibilities under the 1944 Act (as redrafted) and also under the area's five-year development plan. This will involve among other things:
    i) approval each year of each local education authority's educational development plan for primary and secondary education;
    ii) approval each year of local education authority schemes for pupils requiring special educational treatment;
    iii) approval each year of local educational authority schemes for further education; and perhaps the assumption of some direct executive responsibility for the provision of facilities for further education in their areas;

c) maintaining the register of independent schools, arranging for their inspection and taking any necessary executive actions after an inspector's report;

d) producing such ordinances as may be necessary either to:
    i) implement the legislation and policies of the United Kingdom Government and where possible to adapt them to the special needs of their areas; or
    ii) give effect to their residual power to promote the good government and general welfare of the people in their area on educational matters;

e) recommend to the Department of Education such changes in the general educational policy of the U.K. Government as appear to be needed.

Clearly the above functions are substantial – even

> though this comprises a minimum list only. Equally clearly, they are also functions that are best and most advantageously performed at this intermediate level of government. And their devolution to intermediate level governments would greatly relieve the burdens on the Minister of Education and his Department.[22]

It must be said that there are signs that the drafters of this Memorandum of Dissent were a little hazy about aspects of the education system. It is quite simply wrong to say, as they did, that 'the compulsory reorganisation of secondary education on comprehensive lines was imposed by means of a Department of Education Circular 10/65.'[23] Moreover, the need for local authorities to provide educational development plans represents a whole new set of powers, rather than merely the reallocation of powers conferred under the 1944 Act.

But that leads to an important point. It is at least arguable that the proposals in sections (a) and (b) above represent not, for the most part, a devolution of power from the Department so much as the creation of new powers to be exercised at regional or intermediate level. They would represent a *tighter* control and supervision of local authorities than we have at present. Perhaps that is desirable; but it would be the local authorities rather than the central government which would be conscious of a loss of power, and it hardly fits the dissenters' view that 'Local authorities ... could gain substantially from the removal of the now powerful, remote, insensitive hand of Whitehall'.[24] Even the ordinance making power in section (dii) could well result in a limitation of the freedom of local authorities. A specific example of such power given in the Memorandum of Dissent is the right to decide between different types of comprehensive education (given that there has been national legislation making comprehensives compulsory).[25] Under present arrangements, this power would be exercised by local authorities.

The one area of school provision where the regional tier perhaps looks most plausible, is special education Certainly local authorities often do not find it possible to provide a comprehensive range of special schools within their own areas, and co-operation is therefore required between local authorities. The snag here, however, would be that it is generally held desirable to narrow the gap between special schools and ordinary schools, and any further institutionalised separation might be undesirable. In fairness to Lord Crowther-Hunt and Professor Peacock, however, it must be said that they talk only of the approval of plans, and not of their implementation.

But the fundamental question is, of course, whether there is reason to believe that there has been inadequate or excessive school provision because of a failure to link up strategic regional plans with education decisions. That housing and schooling sometimes get out of phase is not disputed; but what the regionalists have to prove is that this is due to failures in large-scale planning as opposed to such things as the fact that a projected housing development may get stuck because of a shortage of materials, manpower, cash or drains; or the notorious tendency of putative parents to fail to deliver the goods in the way that the statisticians expect them to.

If there have been such failures, the question also remains as to whether they need a fully-blown new tier of government to resolve them, or whether a stronger regional administrative set-up would meet the case. As we have seen, the DES has some regional organisation, embracing territorial principals (who however are London-based), regional staff inspectors at regional offices and the RACs. But these are very much education-oriented, rather than engaged in 'interface' with the other regional planning bodies, though the RACs are of course designed to relate to industry's needs in particular. To put it another way, is the educational system's tradition of relatively light, informal administration (anyway above LEA level) outdated in a world of increasingly complex planning and control systems?

CONCLUSIONS

This digest of some of the discussion which has taken place recently on educational organisation and possible regional aspects does not claim to be comprehensive; in particular, it lacks outright advocacy of regionalisation of education. It is moreover particularly slanted towards further education (in the statutory sense and in this context, mainly advanced or higher work). But this reflects what seems to me to be the facts of the situation. There *has* not in fact been much detailed argument of the case for regionalising education or parts of it. At the same time, *prima facie* arguments point to further and higher education (whether including or excluding the universities) as the area in which a case for regional devolution might be most strongly made. At least it is there that such regionalism as there is at present exists. Interestingly enough, the Department of Education and Science – unlike a number of other government departments – did not submit evidence to Kilbrandon; nor did the Association of Education Committees. Indeed the only specifically educational body concerned with English affairs to give evidence was the Committee of Vice-Chancellors and Principals.

It is tempting to tackle the case for educational devolution in two parts: further and higher, on the one hand, and school, on the other. But there is a difficulty about making this distinction, since the statutory further education sector (run by local authorities) embraces both higher or advanced *and* non-advanced work. Clearly it makes little sense to consider organising non-advanced further education work under a separate organisation to that which administers provision for 16–19 year-olds in school; yet it is impossible, at the moment anyway, to draw a sharp divide between advanced and non-advanced work, in that they both take place in many instances within the same colleges of further education. Perhaps with time there could be an absolute division between non-advanced and advanced colleges, and of course the creation of the polytechnics was a substantial move in that direction. Yet there are still large numbers of students doing advanced courses in colleges of further education other than polytechnics and colleges of education. Equally, to carve out a separate 16–19 sector would entail an enormous upheaval in both the school and FE systems.

For the time being, then, it looks as if the only practicable way in which education could be organised regionally would be by bringing it *all* (except perhaps the universities) under the regional government. The regional government would presumably delegate much of the power to the local authorities – indeed all the present powers, if the Kilbrandon emphasis on devolution from the centre, but no transfer of power from local government, were to be upheld. But would this make for a better system then we have at present? Would devolution 'do much to reduce discontent with the system of government'? Would it 'counter over-centralisation and, to a lesser extent strengthen democracy'? Would it in other words meet the Kilbrandon objectives, as set out in their basic conclusion quoted earlier? Would it lighten the load on over-burdened Ministers, MPs and civil servants? And would it – though Kilbrandon was not particularly interested in this sort of question – mean that children and students learned more?

The point to remember in all the arguments about bringing services closer to the public is that education already is for the most part very much a local service. The people who make the bulk of the decisions which affect schools and even colleges are the local authorities or the schools or colleges themselves. LEAs decide whether a child should go to this school or that; and whether (though subject to the Secretary of State) this school or that should exist or be transformed. Meanwhile, the schools (though sometimes strongly influenced by examining boards) determine the curriculum and the style of teaching. Now it is true that the DES has the power to intervene in most of these things in certain circumstances; but this does not alter the fact that the flavour of the educational system is pretty local. There is not much evidence of complaints of over-centralisation: indeed, if anything, the pressure seems towards more centralisation, for example, over comprehensive schools, discretionary grants, and perhaps curricula.

One range of decisions over schools which perhaps might be decentralised are those over building programmes. Obviously there could be regional allocations; as with health, or regions could raise their own money and then direct it as they wished (though given the importance of building as an economic regulator, central government would no doubt be eager to have some say over this). Whether regional governments would make decisions about the allocation of resources much more sensitively than does national government is a matter for conjecture. Moreover, to judge by NHS and other experience, I suspect that many decisions taken on a regional basis are then examined and perhaps even reviewed in London; and that having an extra tier may lead to bureaucracy and slowness. The real problem with building is not the system of allocation but the overall shortage of resources: I know of no evidence that discontent is greater over school building (allocated from London) than over health building (allocated via the regions).

I have argued earlier that a regional tier may more easily serve as a barrier than as a means of avoiding remoteness. People like to feel that the very top is accessible; a regional level *may* make it more distant. With education, the right of an appeal to the Secretary of State may be reassuring: I doubt if appeal to a regional authority would be quite the same thing. Again, even if you have regional government, complaints will continue to go to MPs.

Are MPs too busy to cope with them? I do not myself think so, though I certainly accept that MPs must avoid becoming social workers. And of course they benefit considerably from the contact with everyday problems which their postbags and their 'surgeries' provide. But what about ministers and the DES – are they overburdened to such an extent that education suffers? Obviously secretaries of state and permanent secretaries are very busy; but from my own, admittedly very brief, experience as a junior minister in the DES, I would not say that the burden is damagingly severe. On the ministerial side it may be possible to lift more of it by delegation to junior ministers. That option is available to secretaries of state who feel they have too much on their plate.

What would be very damaging would be so to devolve power that ministers and officials at the DES lost all direct contact with what goes on in the schools and colleges. Examining school reorganisation proposals; individual complaints about school places; local authority building representatations; compulsory purchase orders; visiting schools and receiving delegations, are all excellent ways of preventing Elizabeth House becoming an ivory tower. Parliamentary questions on matters of details (which would be ruled out of court under devolved government) serve the same purpose. And would the Expenditure Committee be restricted in its investigations by devolution?

On the whole, then, the balance between national and local decision making, loosely defined though it in some ways is, does not seem to make for a feeling that democracy or accessibility are lacking. One may hear the complaint that the education authority is too remote, in some counties particularly. But this comes from those who regret the passing of some smaller authorities or of the divisional executives: it certainly does not express a hankering after regionalism.

The only area of school education which seems to offer a case for regionalisation is special education, where institutions for children with some uncommon handicaps like autism or perhaps extreme maladjustment are not necessary or anyway feasible in every local educational authority. But with the increasing emphasis on avoiding a sharp divide between special and ordinary education it would be foolish to separate provision for them; while to base the whole pattern of school administration on the needs of handicapped children would be strange.

Perhaps this is unfair. What the regionalists really want tends to be control over planning and supervision rather than actual execution of policy. As I have already pointed out, Kilbrandon says that the regions 'might become responsible for the general supervision of local education authorities, including the inspection of schools, for the grant of all approvals of development plans and of schemes of provision for primary, secondary, further and special education, and for the control of capital investment.'[26] The regionalists would argue, moreover, that all these powers would be transferred from the Department; that the local authorities would be left with all their present functions. In theory this is probably so; in practice once a regional government had been set up it would be likely to seek to extend its power. The notion that planning and supervision can be left at that is as yet unproven. Moreover, there could obviously be complications if the national-regional-local system produced different political parties in control at each level – say Labour at national, Tory at regional and Liberal at local. To have different parties at national and local level may bring advantages as well as drawbacks. But to have *three* different policies could be altogether too much.

When we look at further and higher education, the position is complicated by the fact that provision for 16–19 year-olds takes place in both schools and further education colleges, and further education colleges provide both advanced and non-advanced work. As we have seen already, a variety of complaints exist about the present system. To those may be added a dislike on the part of local authorities of the pooling system for higher education. There is also a conflict between the view that higher education fulfils a national role and should therefore be organised on that basis and the view that higher education should be more closely linked (locally and regionally) with the needs of industry, commerce and other employment.

From all this two principal alternatives to the present system seem to emerge: greater co-ordination of the two systems of higher education; and the planning of non-university higher education on a wider basis than the LEA unit. As to the former, however, the argument seems to an extent to be a question of co-ordination at *national* level, through, for example, a single Higher Education Committee, which would effectively control the universities and the polytechnics, or a Polytechnics Grants Committee. I have my doubts about this, but this is not essentially a question about regionalism. I find the Vice-Chancellors' evidence in favour of a national rather than a regionalised system of universities persuasive.

On the latter, it seems that the case for some strengthened regional system seems reasonable, so as to produce better use of the resources of polytechnics, colleges of education, and other further education institutions; to improve liaison with the universities and to have contact with industry and the economic sphere. But should this go beyond the enlargement of the scope of the Regional Advisory Councils? Presumably, there is a likelihood that as a result of the present review the RACs and the ATOs will move closer together and perhaps be fused; but the signs are that the DES intends to continue to have the ultimate say over courses.

Would this be better devolved to a regional government? Again, it clearly could be. But I suspect that the regional government would find that national considerations related to overall standards and qualifications, manpower planning, and finance would constantly hamstring it, and it would be contrary to the Kilbrandon philosophy of devolution to start removing substantial power from below (the LEAs) in the actual management of the colleges. This could be done – perhaps at the same time as giving the colleges greater autonomy. But overall I doubt if further and higher education really needs a regional government tier for the solution of its problems. Moreover, there could be significant losses in a break of the link between schools and further education colleges, or between the non-higher further education colleges and the higher further education colleges (particularly as colleges combine both). Apart from anything else, adult and continuing education could suffer somewhat from a separation of the two. At the same time, anything that took the 16–19 age group away from the LEAs could make it often impossible to manage the education of that age group to the best advantage. Regionalisation of further and higher education could in fact probably only proceed on the basis of a sharp break between advanced and non advanced institutions.

In summary, therefore, school education seems to me to stand to gain nothing from regional devolution in England. Nor does non-advanced further education work require more than a small amount of inter-LEA collaboration. Higher education obviously could be run on a regional basis; the present system, particularly over colleges of education, is rightly under review. But some sort of strengthened advisory system should be able to meet the case, and there would be drawbacks in transferring the colleges from the LEAs (though arguably the polytechnics should be run on national lines, comparable to the UGC system). The universities are better left as a national tier.

NOTES AND REFERENCES

1 Royal Commission on the Constitution, *Devolution and Other Aspects of Government: An Attitudes Survey*, Research Paper 7 (HMSO, 1973).
2 Expenditure Committee, Session 1972–3, *Further and Higher Education*, vol. II (HMSO, 1973) p. 10.
3 J. A. G. Griffith, *Central Departments and Local Authorities* (George Allen and Unwin, 1966).
4 *Report of the Royal Commission on Local Government in England*, Cmnd. 4040–1, vols. I and II (HMSO, 1969).
5 Ibid., para. 419.
6 Ibid., para. 420.
7 *Kilbrandon Report*, p. 484, conclusion 170.
8 Ibid., para. 709.
9 Ibid., para. 841.
10 Ibid., para. 871.
11 *Memorandum of Dissent*, Appendix C, para. 22.
12 *Kilbrandon Report*, Appendix D, para. 71.
13 Royal Commission on the Constitution, *Written Evidence 9: United Kingdom* (HMSO, 1972), p. 21.
14. Expenditure Committee, op. cit., vol. I, p. xxi.

15 Ibid., vol. II, p. 11.
16 Ibid., vol. I, p. xxiv.
17 Ibid.
18 Department of Education and Science, *Education: A Framework for Expansion*, Cmnd. 5174 (HMSO, 1972) para. 87.
19 Department of Education and Science, *Teacher Education and Training: Report of Committee of Inquiry* (HMSO, 1972).
20 Ibid., para. 529.
21 See Department of Education and Science Circular 6/74.
22 *Memorandum of Dissent*, Appendix C, para. 42.
23 Ibid., Appendix C, para. 11.
24 Ibid., Appendix C, para. 22.
25 Ibid., para. 218(f).
26 *Kilbrandon Report*, para. 871.

4 Regional Devolution and the Personal Social Services

KENNETH URWIN

THE PRESENT ARRANGEMENTS

The personal social services in Britain are in the main a compound of local authority action and central government suasion. Thus, unlike the services most closely related to them (the income support agencies and – outside Scotland – the probation service), they revolve around the axis which links two kinds of democratic body; the citizen is concerned both as taxpayer and ratepayer; and the quality of the services is determined by the interaction of initiatives taken centrally and locally. The case for regional devolution, in any one of its manifestations, rests upon the assertion that the initiatives taken are not enough – or that the bodies responsible for taking the initiatives are malfunctioning and need to be replaced.

The duties and powers under which the local authorities do their work comprise some twenty statutes and a long list of statutory instruments. The Local Authorities Social Services Act 1970, with its counterpart for Scotland in the Social Work (Scotland) Act 1968, required an explicit organisation–social services or social work committees and departments in every relevant local authority. But they did not and could not command an explicit objective. For there is no single concretely expressible objective which bears on all the vulnerable people with whom a social services authority is concerned. There is no one form of words which characterises the quality of a local authority's intervention in matters so broad as parent–child relationships, or so contentious as the treatment owed to deviant, rootless and ineffectual persons, or so complex and onerous as the provision made for the mentally ill, mentally handicapped, physically handicapped and elderly.

The canons of social services authorities include, first, accessibility; second, maximum flexibility in practice and the avoidance of any standard formula; and third, a consequent freedom, in any individual case of need, to take action *ad hoc* without having to justify it in every detail by reference to standard rules. These canons imply a type of organisation which, without prejudice to effective overall policy and management, will adequately delegate to locally based personnel extensive responsibilities in day-to-day decision-making.

The present structure of the services thus reflects at once a division of functions and a delicate balance of interests between central and local government. Their planning and delivery are tasks vested in the local authorities – over a hundred of them – who as well as statutory mandates have significant discretionary powers: the power to receive or not receive children into care, for example. Government departments for their part, pre-eminently the Department of Health and Social Security, the Department of the Environment, the Welsh and the Scottish Offices, and the Treasury, stimulate, inhibit and qualify the local authorities' activities. They exercise this function chiefly by determining the amount of rate support grant awarded annually to local government as a whole, and the formula by which the grant is distributed among authorities by reference to their resources and needs. Social services expenditure needs are taken into account for this purpose, but the grant itself is a 'block' grant and thus not earmarked for any particular service. Capital expenditure in the provision of new buildings is largely financed by borrowing, and this has to be approved by the Department of Health and Social Security or its Welsh and Scottish counterparts, since it also has important revenue effects – partly because the repayments and interest form an annual charge on the rates, and partly because new projects connote new running expenses. In these ways, although central government cannot directly control local authority rate levels, it can in practice find ways to influence trends in local authority spending, on these as on other services. Thus, through the Secretary of State for the Social Services, the government has stated that from 1975–6 local authorities will be free to determine their own priorities in expenditure, within the constraints imposed by national economic and social priorities.[1] With rate support grant based on a planned growth rate restricted in real terms to 2.7 per cent per annum up to 1978–9, the local authorities are urged to give special emphasis to certain fields of their work, but otherwise left to their own initiative in determining the direction of their momentum—on which they have already indicated their broad intentions in their ten-year plans. Central government in the DHSS and Scottish and Welsh Offices maintains a watching brief over how they actually operate, through the Social Work Service – which is divided up regionally for organisational convenience and more effective local contact.

The predicted total expenditure on the local authority personal social services for 1975–6 is £647 million (as compared with an actual level of expenditure of £343 million in 1969–70). Central and miscellaneous costs shared with the health service are calculated at £99 million. As background it has to be noted that income support payments through the Supplementary Benefits Commission are estimated to total £786 million for the same year; the probation service is likely to cost £35 million; and several millions will be spent on social service provision of one kind or another by voluntary organisations. Probably some 15–20 per cent of the population at any one time is currently receiving direct support from one or more of the personal social services. Comparative figures of expenditure forecast for 1975–6 in adjacent areas of the public sector are, in education and libraries, science and arts, £4624 million (actual expenditure 1969–70, £3674 million); in the health service, £3283 million (1969–70, £2679 million); in housing, £3317 million (1969–70, £2181 million).[2]

The probation service, as a component element of the country's judicial processes, owes its governmental allegiance in England and Wales to the Home Office and the Welsh Office. It has very restricted spending powers. The voluntary organisations, despite the independence their title connotes, carry a most important recognition within the statutory framework of provision, either because central or local government may offer them direct grant for specific projects (for example, for the care of drug addicts), or because of official powers of inspection (over a voluntary home for deprived children, for instance). The Supplementary Benefits Commission is a civil service cash-dispensing organisation controlled by a body of nine appointed commissioners directly accountable to central government.

It will be apparent that the main thrust of change has been developed within the local authority field. The Seebohm Committee, whose report precipitated the Local Authorities Social Services Act 1970, argued the case for a reorganisation of social provision so that the services might:

a) meet needs on the basis of the overall requirements of the individual or family rather than on the basis of a limited set of symptoms;
b) provide a clear and comprehensive pattern of responsibility over the whole field;
c) attract more resources;
d) use those resources more effectively;
e) generate adequate recruitment and training of the staff skills which are, or may become necessary;
f) meet needs which are at present being neglected;
g) adapt to changing conditions;
h) provide a better organisation for collecting and disseminating information relevant to the development of the social services;
i) be more accessible and comprehensible to those who need to use them.[3]

In the light of this large perspective, the Seebohm Committee proposed a restructuring of local authority services for England and Wales calculated to be 'effective within a dynamic democratic local government system'. The report went on:

> For those it is intended to serve, 'effectiveness' implies a service which is accessible and acceptable and which meets the need promptly, that is, a service which is as far as possible community based. 'Effectiveness' in terms of the service offered implies one which had adequate skills to cope with needs; sufficient manpower to maintain the service under all conditions; comprehensive training facilities to provide a progressive and expanding service, and a wide variety of physical resources to support the field

> workers. 'Effectiveness' in terms of democratically controlled local government service implies a service with assured communication between the 'consumer' of the service and those responsible for policy and for provision of the necessary resources.[4]

In consequence, the Seebohm Committee emphasised the importance of an 'area' grouping of social workers within the local authority – to provide, in towns, for a population of between 50,000 and 100,000 people. These 'area teams', being close to the residents of the neighbourhood they served, should have relative independence of judgement and action in undertaking their tasks. Specialist staff like occupational therapists, together with home helps and other social service aides, could also be based in the area. In close relationship with these area social worker teams were to be day care and residential establishments using, so far as practicable, the area as catchment zone. Very particular types of service which are perennially in short supply, such as various forms of day and residential provision for socially handicapped children, were always assumed to be associated with a much wider locality than the area.

The following groups are in practice those which have the main access to one or more forms of personal social service provision:

a) families with children under five (in respect of a variety of forms of pre-school care);
b) families with children and young persons under 18 (in respect of provision under several statutes concerned with this age group);
c) the homeless;
d) the mentally ill;
e) the mentally handicapped;
f) the physically handicapped;
g) the elderly.

The voluntary element apart, and this element has no significant stake in the regionalist controversy, there is substantial variation in the outlay on services of separate local authorities, and thus in their quality and coverage.

Given these arrangements and the circumstances in which they have developed, any case for regional devolution considered in 1975 must take into account the fluidity of present relationships between the Department of Health and Social Security and the local social services authorities. There has been no time, after so comprehensive an organisational change, for mutually felt tensions to be resolved, nor for the earliest and very tentative working patterns created by the new Act to settle into a constructive network of relationships.

The regional proposals which have actually been made in relation to the social services seem likely to presage either a consultative and a co-ordinating regional organisation, set midway between central and local government, or a stronger legislative or executive regional organisation taking away a majority of the powers of central government and some from the local authorities. This distinction follows broadly the lines of debate between the majority of the Kilbrandon Committee and the two members who subscribed to the Memorandum of Dissent. Yet whether any regional structure is essentially of a consultative or an executive kind, a further decision will have to be taken in social services matters: shall the remit of such a body include all matters currently referred to social services committees or be confined to particular mandates, perhaps in areas of work where the task of making provision is most specialised, or where community resources are in the shortest supply?

THE DEVOLUTIONISTS' PROPOSALS: CONSULTATIVE COUNCILS

The Kilbrandon Report itself states:

> It is a function of DHSS to ensure the provision by local authorities and voluntary agencies in England of personal social services under the Local Authority Social Services Act 1970 and other social service legislation. The services include the care in the community of the mentally disordered, the physically handicapped, the elderly and the homeless; the care and protection of children; and provision for the socially inadequate, including alcoholics and drug addicts. Local authorities are required to discharge their responsibilities in accordance with any guidance given by the Secretary of State. The department's Social Work Service provides professional advice in the discharge of these functions, and through its regional organisation offers

support to local authorities, monitors their performance and informs the department of needs and developments in the field.

The Welsh Office administers the social services in Wales. In Scotland separate legislation on social work is administered by the Scottish Office through its Social Work Services Group; social work departments in local authorities provide an integrated service which covers probation and after-care in addition to the personal social services. Children's hearings have replaced juvenile courts in Scotland and deal with children in need of compulsory care and supervision, including most juvenile offenders; the hearings are organised by local authorities and serviced by their social work departments. Devolution of these functions would be possible.[5]

It is necessary, for a start, to qualify the Report's reference to the function of the Department of Health and Social Security in England, and the Welsh Office in Wales, 'to *ensure* the provision by local authorities and voluntary agencies of personal social services'. In fact, central government in England and Wales has only a limited capacity to carry out this function. It provides only a limited proportion of the financial resources which local authorities must raise (in London no more than one quarter); and it gives minimally to the voluntary organisations. The local authorities and voluntary bodies for their part value their degree of autonomy. Thus the Report's turn of phrase in this section suggests a degree of over-valuation of central government's role.

The Report goes on to argue the practicability of regional devolution in the functions allotted to central government, and a majority of the Commission's members offer a case for regional, partly elected, partly nominated bodies – consultative, advisory, certainly non-legislative, non-executive – which might constitute an intermediate tier in the decision-making processes linking central and local government (see Scheme F in the appendix). Except at the evaluative level, it is difficult to see how this sort of regional intervention can be very relevant to the social services. It adds nothing to provision and would only doubtfully lead to a more effective or equitable distribution of existing resources.

As prototypes of regional organisations with limited scope

and limited objective, there have already been the Children's Regional Planning Committees set up as an adjunct to the Children and Young Persons Act of 1969. These Committees would seem to have served as little more than an *aide-mémoire* to local authorities, in eleven different regions of England and Wales, of their responsibilities in the creation and the maintenance of community homes. Ostensibly the Committees are a device intended to create, from within the separate resources of the constituent local authorities, a broad structure of provision for young people who are in trouble as offenders. The local authority representatives on the Committee resolve to accept principles of admission whereby boys and girls can be found places in more sought-after units of care – in particular, observation and assessment centres. Now the arrangements made may be valuable and economical, but they remain at the level of a working agreement, with no injunction to the participating local authorities which carries the force of a mandate or a requirement. Central government uses the Committees in an advisory role when it needs to determine the loan sanctions available to individual local authorities for their capital programmes. The existence of the Committees may have sharpened the facility of local authority spokesmen for appraising what provision they and their neighbours make for children and adolescents in care. Equally it may have served as an unnecessary check on some local authorities when they seek to construct a coherent programme for young offenders within or close to their own geographical boundaries. But that is all. Regional planning committees have not been set up in other sectors of the social services. Their establishment would give rise to similarly varied questions as are raised in the case of community homes, and the answer to those questions would not indicate clear-cut gain.

Given the type of regional structure proposed by the majority of the Kilbrandon Commission, it is important to recognise what would remain to be done – over and above the regional body's operations. Local authorities would still have to fulfil their statutory duties and exercise their statutory powers; voluntary organisations would still have to maintain their own particular *locus*. The raising of revenue for local authority activities would still remain a contractual obligation between central and local government. The wide variations in outlay on social provision per head of population in different parts of Britain would not alter.

Though regional councils could become a useful forum for astringent criticism of standards in social provision, they could not regulate the pressure of work in separate local authorities, nor could they monitor its effect. So a considered judgement must be that the case for regional consultative councils is thin and – in the circumstances of severely restricted resources – unduly costly. Whatever happens in the field of regional devolution, any machinery set up for regional consultation could not be allowed to replace the exercise of functions which properly and inevitably must reside in central government; and it is also unrealistic to assume the availability of personnel to make the regional council structures effective.

Some might see special merits in the idea of regional consultative councils in the following special types of case:

i) where there is arguably a ceiling imposed on the material resources available to meet an overt need, like the need of people and families for a home, and where regional bodies may *prima facie* seem an appropriate device to encourage the sharing of limited assets and ensure that these assets are used to maximum advantage;
ii) where the work of local authorities impinges most closely on the restructured national health service – notably in provision made for the mentally ill and mentally handicapped.

In these two areas of work, the statutory task certainly needs intensive inter-authority *collaboration*; and it is possible to compare the principles and premises of action which apply in these two matters with those obtaining in a third, namely, the support of families with young children under pressure, which is recognisably a very localised responsibility. This comparison is made later in this chapter; but the case for even consultative councils at regional level still does not emerge as very much stronger.

THE DEVOLUTIONISTS' PROPOSALS: SUBSTANTIVE DEVOLUTION

Under the fullest type of devolution to regional bodies, each such body would have a separate corpus of social statute, its own revenue-raising powers, and general planning powers, together with specific controls over the delivery of services by the region's local authorities.

In a word, the impact of these regional bodies on the local authorities would be far more pervasive than that of central government now. Unlike mere regional consultative and co-ordinative councils of the kind discussed earlier, they would have real power to push for further resources from central government and to require particular ranges or patterns of service from the local authorities.

And herein lies the basic difficulty. For in the twentieth century, the personal social services have become, with education and housing, the spinal cord of *local* government, and this argues tellingly against both the concept of regional organisation sprouting from the grass roots upwards and that of regional devolution in the sense of central government functions transferred to a dozen other governments scattered across England and Wales. Statutory duties and powers now vested in local authorities become most cogent and binding when they enable their elected members to stay close to the people. The regional counter-proposal which would either withdraw the elected representative from the people by requiring him to serve on a regional body, or strip the local authority of its valuable discretionary powers, will in practice be countenanced only in extremis.

So, short of war, earthquake and famine, for which conditions the Royal Commission was not making recommendations, it has to be asked what remotely conceivable national situation could justify the regional proposals? First, there would need to be intense disenchantment which could only reflect flagrant inefficiency in both kinds of government, or excessively long lines of communication. Secondly, local authorities would need forthwith to reject expansionist projects in the field of social provision, deliberately refusing further to extend the *quantum* of the population on whose behalf personal social services are argued for. Thirdly, the groundswell of discontent would have to be fomented at local level by disaffected activists, and channelled into avowedly regionalist alternatives, with particular emphasis on the right of the regions to levy and distribute their own revenues (and presumably income support functions currently vested in the Supplementary Benefits Commission would be seen as a natural component of the regional package). Finally, local authorities would have to abrogate all their social planning and certain of their delivery functions in favour of a regional authority.

There is in fact no reason why such a combination of circumstances and attitudes should be assumed or allowed to exist. The personal social services are among the kinds of community provision which people continue to regard as requiring the maximum of localised planning and delivery, responsive to localised pressures exerted through locally accountable elected bodies, though within the context of general national policies. The kinds of substantive devolution proposals described in the Kilbrandon Report and especially its Memorandum of Dissent, even if they do not include legislative devolution, would in practice be as destructive of that genuinely localised power and responsiveness as they would be of the effective power of the central government itself.

THE IRRELEVANCE OF REGIONALISM

The fact is that the case for regional devolution, whenever advanced, is in essence political, resting on value judgements made about the region as a cultural grouping. In the field of the personal social services, the case depends on the proposition that the people receiving or delivering them can be meaningfully perceived and catered for in a regional rather than a national and local framework. The functional case is secondary and derivative.

Yet in practice it is difficult to see in what ways overall regional intervention – except in highly specialised fields like the hospitals and perhaps some higher education establishments – will add efficiency to the planning or administration of existing services of this kind. Even given the fact that limited social resources have to be equitably distributed through the country, and that local authorities as the providing bodies have to be accountable for their joint organisation, no units of care are to be found in the personal social services where the arguments for specialist, therefore highly differentiated, therefore regional provision outweigh the advantages of local availability and local delivery. And this judgement is not vitiated by the decision of the Department of Health and Social Security itself to set up, on the basis of broadly regional catchment areas, a few treatment centres for very disturbed and deviant adolescents; there is always a case for the experimental project which breaks the norm, and a pilot scheme can be directly sponsored and controlled by central government as much as by a private or voluntary body.

Certainly the Department of Health and Social Security, as an organ of state, does not at present find it necessary to delegate its functions to autonomous regional structures. It merely bases certain of its personnel in different parts of the country – chiefly Social Work Service officers – for purposes of monitoring; the Welsh Office meets that need for the social services in Wales; and though the legislative framework in Scotland is different, the Scottish Office has a not dissimilar function north of the border.

Admittedly the Supplementary Benefits Commission, with a complex political ancestry, allows itself a regional structure interposed between its central and its local administration, to serve as a staging point in the Commission's own communication system. It is responsible for the administration of central policy within the region, and reflects back from local offices the effect of policy edicts. But line management from local offices through the region to a London-based headquarters ensures the minimum of autonomy at any point in the network; and to the average member of the public the regional level of the Commission is about as significant as the road to Samarkand.

These regional organisations, both set up within the extensive orbit of the Department of Health and Social Security, are officer constructions within the Civil Service. They do not mirror any regional differences of culture or environment. For example, they do not to any notable degree relate issues of regional unemployment or under-employment with the functions of social service agencies. Because they comprise teams of civil servants, there is no attachment of nominated or elected regional members. Yet even if there were a regional organisation on a different and democratic footing – a statutorily recognised regional council reporting back to Westminster and Whitehall, perhaps to Cardiff – it is doubtful whether such a body would ever speak to any effect. The reasons for its inhibitions are found in the character of social provision in this country and elsewhere in the Western world, and the kind of issues with which the social services deal. These reasons in themselves require the *local* authority to be articulate; there must be communication between *local* councils and central government. But there is very little room – or need – for a regional voice as well.

For at the delivery level, what is of primary importance is closeness between the parties to social provision. One of the big difficulties in social services administration is that comparatively few who are practitioners in this field have ever been at the receiving end of the services they offer; at a random guess, perhaps 1 in 1000. That power to criticise organisations and structure which derives its authenticity from personal experience of face-to-face encounter with officialdom is therefore lacking. Care for the severely dependent and insecure is offered by those who have not known severe dependence or insecurity. All this makes for potential misunderstanding of what is needed and how to deliver it. It is the source of insensitive value judgements common to those functioning at whatever level of government is involved. But these adverse effects of the polarisation of the practitioner from the recipient of social services can at all events be minimised by the existence of effective power, close at hand, in the person of the properly critical *local* elected representative. He can take responsibility for what is under or close to his own eye. A regional authority cannot.

At the broad policy level, the profound issues which are implicit in the notion of community-based support to vulnerable individuals do of course have a more than local – indeed a national – dimension. But is very questionable whether they have a regional dimension too. There is extensive public credulity about the objectives, the character and the extent of British social servies. As with the infant medical profession centuries ago, too much is expected of practitioners who are groping their way. Reassuring answers are sought by members of the public to nationally framed questions which betray their anxiety. Why cannot the child thief be taught to respect our property values? Why cannot the elderly endure their poverty, and their under-heated rooms? Somehow a national and a local answer has to be provided to such questions – national as reflecting general societal attitudes, local as reflecting their practical interpretation. But there seems little point in a regional answer as well.

In so far as the social services are redistributive in character, there will be a point at which redistribution abruptly stops. The Treasury and the local authority councillor may vie with each other over the accuracy of their judgement about the tolerance level of the taxpayer and the ratepayer. But the see-saw action involves central and local government alone: it is the sign and token of the varying resource demands made on the citizen. There is no case for a regional body to be associated with the feat of balancing the two kinds of demand.

Then there is the matter of actual delivery method. And here practitioners themselves tend to eschew the large-scale social service organisation. They admit that the social services of Britain are a complex skein of over-provision and under-provision. A substantial element in the adult population – perhaps one in five persons – remains a victim of distributive inequities, and for people in this minority group the character of the governmental organisation which may meet their claims is a perennial subject for controversy. But many practitioners, professionally trained social workers among them, are much less impressed in their thinking by the large region concept than by that of the neighbourhood or village society. Within the narrow perimeter of that kind of area – perhaps only a quarter-mile radius in a closely populated city – resources are measurable; and to be able to measure resources brings its own reassurance. One knows by acquaintance and instinct those residents with time, energy and competence to care for the lost child, the single-parent family, the frail elderly. At this level there is always a working summary of resources. A twentieth-century feudal society would have inordinately large claims on the affection of social workers.

It is possible, of course, for social practitioners to hypnotise themselves into an unreal myopic state where nothing matters except their reaction to zombie creatures in a tiny island of time and space. An unresolved tension in the personal social services is the solipsism of social workers. However, this tension, and others with it, is not removed by a regional solution. Any predilection for micro-politics has nothing to do with regionalism. All it argues is a naive distrust of central government, perhaps of the larger units of local government also, and a naive zest for delegation. Every social agency is under pressure from its own workers to see an increased range of planning and executive functions entrusted to locally based personnel. From their point of view the unacceptability of regional proposals in any shape or form is absolute; for regionalism cannot win the political assent it needs from those whose only ambition is to serve as a walking neighbourhood centre. This in itself, of course, cannot be a decisive argument, but on the other hand the likely view of those who actually have to deliver the personal social services in the field cannot be ignored.

One side-glance at contemporary social history may be permitted. In England, a former quasi-regional authority in the shape of the London County Council, though technically a unique local authority, yielded the social service function to the newly created London boroughs in 1965. A social historian, E. B. Wistrich, records her impression of this centrifugal operation:

> Most Camden officers were sure that they had improved their service to the public by providing a more local service, responsive to community needs, and a well co-ordinated one. Their judgment is probably true. The LCC was organised into large operating units with too remote a bureaucracy to be as close to the ground as Camden Council.
>
> The transfer of the three social services from the LCC was initially viewed with great concern by many who admired the LCC services. Great fears were expressed about the likely fall in standards of provision and of administration. Professor David Donnison, for example, feared that to provide certain existing services or make any major improvements, there would either have to be increased central government intervention or a reform of the local government structure to allow bigger groupings of London boroughs. Great opposition was mounted by the Labour party to the transfer of the children's service and this opposition was supported by several professional bodies. An experienced critic feared that the boroughs would be less likely to undertake experiment and research in the children's service. The evidence of experience in Camden shows that in one borough at least these fears were unfounded. Services were not only sustained at the previous levels, but in many instances developed and improved. Innovation was frequent, and there were far

closer contacts with other local institutions such as hospitals than in LCC days. Many more day and residential establishments were built within the Borough boundaries, close to the areas where people had family and neighbourhood contacts. It is true that Camden was the third wealthiest London authority (after Westminster and the City) and thus able to finance good quality services and new ventures in its areas of greater need. But it is also true that the Council took advantage of its opportunities to build up the services and was able to justify the claim that they were far closer to the community than they had been under the LCC.[6]

In Scotland from 1975 onwards the converse argument will be put forward. Seven regional local authorities will effectively replace smaller local authority organisations. It has yet to be seen from that experience what merit can attach to the dissolution of executive responsibility at the really local level.

It may be argued that although all this may serve as a warning against regional bodies taking personal social services powers away from local authorities – or interfering too much in the way they exercise them – it does not dispose of the case for regional bodies to exercise some of the responsibilities in respect of personal social services which are currently vested in central government in Whitehall. But it is the contention of this chapter that, given the characteristics and needs of the personal social services as described above, there is very little that a regional body could do about them except take powers away from the local level, because the limited powers operated at the national level are entirely of a national nature; there is no room for anything significant in between. Indeed, the interposition of an additional government level could be positively counter-productive, let it get its powers from whence it might, for what is urgently needed in the personal social services is not a diversion of energy to an irrelevant new set of authorities but a more vigorous approach to problems already waiting to be tackled at the level where they arise and can alone be dealt with: locally. Let us consider some examples.

A TEST CASE: PROVISION FOR THE HOMELESS

Least attractive of all the elements of social under-provision, homelessness is now an endemic sore in the United Kingdom.

It is precipitated by low-key housing programmes which reflect an inaccurate reading of population trends or patterns of migration. It is the other face of unemployment, which often drives the workless into improvident searches for a job in distant and already overcrowded conurbations, especially London. In the view of some, it is aggravated by the unreadiness of a libertarian government in peace-time to requisition spare housing resources: privately owned properties stand empty while the homeless lack a roof over their heads. In England and Wales the number of families officially declared homeless on 31 March 1974 was 8021, of whom 4721 were in the Greater London area.[7] This figure ignores the squatters, the illegal sub-tenants, the families sheltering with friends or neighbours. Pre-eminently, to provide for homeless people is the function of housing authorities which either possess or seek to acquire the means to allot a unit of accommodation to those genuinely deprived of it. Housing authorities in England and Wales, with the exception of the GLC, are all organised on a district, i.e. local authority, basis and not a regional basis. The provision made may be either short-term accommodation or a continuous tenancy. It will be made for persons and families, the majority of whom have been resident or traceable within the local authority's boundaries for a substantial period of time. The experience of one London aurthority (Camden) is not atypical. Of the homeless families admitted in a year, 43 per cent were formerly borough-based – right up to the moment of their seeking aid; 12 per cent came directly from Eire and 6 per cent from Northern Ireland; 7 per cent had former addresses in Scotland and the North of England; 24 per cent in London and the Home Counties.[8]

The homeless have in common only their deprivation of shelter. A social services authority is involved notably because of the multiple pressures exerted on the homeless – in particular the nomadic minority who have no evident association with the authority where they first declared themselves homeless. This latter element in the population, with or without children, lacks roots, tends to wander indiscriminately, and makes predictable demands upon social resources in the area where temporarily it is domiciled. The adults in this heterogeneous group may not stay in any one place long enough to be recognised as earning their keep.

They tend to be categorised broadly as non-contributory drones, whereas investigation suggests that in fact they include a high proportion of migrant workers seeking settlement. They have a plethora of intensifying personal difficulties.

In the conurbations, *ad hoc* proposals for a regional structure to cope with the homeless have been canvassed, even when divorced from all other governmental structures. Local authorities have the largest possible fear of the imposition on their rate resources of the cost of transit camps in perpetuity. They know too that the homeless are queue-jumping.

Defensively, it has been suggested that central government should assume direct responsibility for the homeless by setting up regional organisations based in city areas, especially in London. The argument fails, as it must, at the point where local authorities have to declare what proportion of their housing stock they would yield to the new organisation. Boroughs in the outer conurbations, i.e. commuter territory, have little taste for regional structure to relieve homelessness. Policy-makers in inner city areas are ambivalent about the surrender of their difficult freedom of action. Central government therefore resigns itself to exhortation. The Joint Circular of February 1974 states:

> Where the problems of homelessness bear more heavily on one district than another, help for the homeless can most effectively be provided only when the authorities co-operate to share the burden. This is particularly the case in Greater London and there the GLC use their position and wide housing powers to help. But the incidence of homelessness can be unequal also in the metropolitan counties and in some groups of districts outside them. Where the problem of homelessness bears with undue weight on a few authorities it needs to be shared.[9]

However it is beyond argument that separate local authorities are arbitrary in their treatment of the homeless. John Greve writes:

> Even allowing for the extent to which collaboration between boroughs has developed since 1965, our study has shown that there is still an excessive amount of arbitrariness in policies, and that this influences people's chances

of having their problems dealt with as well as the form of assistance they may receive. This arbitrariness is largely determined by the degree to which officers and councillors formulate and execute policies (involving defining needs and allocating resources) as if a borough's boundaries delineated some real and balanced geographical distribution of needs and resources.[10]

These are salient points. Local authorities when they fail collectively to deliver the goods in a crucial area of social provision must also be collectively answerable for the degree of inequity in provision to which vulnerable people in different parts of the country are subject. However, it is questionable whether the task of matching people to limited resources can ever be free from some element of randomness. Who from the city, denuded of housing opportunity, goes to the overspill areas, the new towns? Certainly not those who can settle there. County authorities are notably apprehensive about the export from the conurbation of a high proportion of families who prove immediately frustrated by the experience, even though they have a tenancy to their name.

Accordingly the prospects of basing provision for the homeless on a regional structure do not seem very hopeful. And any proposals for doing so would meet the following difficulties in particular:

i) in a regional body there is no likelihood that the actual allocation of tenancies will be more effective or more equitable;
ii) prospective tenants will rarely opt for a regional solution if it requires them to live away from the environment to which they are attached;
iii) those who speak for and practise in areas where pressure is highest will make different responses to the homelessness predicament from those where pressure is less intense.

If central government with the force of national will and resources behind it has not, cannot or will not overcome these obstacles, why should it be thought that regional authorities enjoying fragmented central power but themselves subject to the stresses described, would do any better?

A TEST CASE: PROVISION FOR THE MENTALLY ILL AND MENTALLY HANDICAPPED

Care for the mentally disordered is a second area of work in which it is specially relevant to review the organisational principles of effective provision. The mentally ill and the mentally handicapped must have access to in-patient hospital provision. They also must live – a majority of them – in the community. Local authorities servicing hospitals with social workers and making available day care or residential care resources for the mentally disordered outside the hospital seek to balance the twin elements in their task. Very considerable emphasis attaches to community care. The proportion of in-patients in psychiatric hospitals or hospitals for the mentally handicapped who, given access to tangible supports in the community, could function outside the hospitals' structure, may be as high as one in three. As a corollary, given similar community supports, proportionately fewer persons with a diagnosed mental illness or acknowledged mental handicap might require admission to hospitals in the first place.

The policy-maker in the social services field confronted with a health service to which a regional element has become integral will inevitably explore how far the responsibilities of agencies in providing for the mentally disordered can be met by a similar structure. It is fairly axiomatic in the principles underlying the health service that regional arrangements are validated by the incidence of highly specialist work in the hospital field. But the organisational premises of health provision are that it is the *district* hospitals' responsibilities that must include the in-patient treatment of the mentally ill and perhaps of the mentally handicapped. Accordingly collaboration at the interface between health and social services does not require identical regional structures. The boundaries of local authorities and health areas or districts are aligned, and that is enough to provide the groundwork for effective consultation and co-operation between the two types of agency.

Since the reorganisation of the health service in 1974 it has been a statutory function of local authorities to provide hospitals and clinics, including hospitals or wards for the mentally disordered, with social work support. In effect, a social worker team is now seconded from local authorities to the health service, carrying responsibilities within the perimeter of the hospital and where appropriate following up patients needing community care. These groups of social workers have to practise a dual accountability – to the health clinical team of which they form part, and to their own parent local authority. Hospital catchment areas are not coterminous with the dimensions of local authorities. Integration between the social workers attached to each hospital is therefore specially important, for patients may be in hospital away from their local authority's field of responsibility. National hospitals in particular will be accommodating patients irrespective of their home location: a social worker in a London borough, for example, may sometimes be involved via a national hospital with patients of whom only 1 in 25 come from addresses within that borough's area. And in the specific field of provision for the mentally disordered, one local authority's social workers may have to act, initially at least, for several authorities. But this situation does not present undue difficulties.

However, a much larger issue is whether regional health authorities on the one hand, and individual local authorities on the other, can present to the Department of Health and Social Security equally cogent cases for hospital provision and community provision (in the shape of day care or residential care units). Both types of organisation are in fact making a simultaneous claim on limited capital resources. All the machinery for decision-making in central government's allocation to the health service and the social services is vested in the Department, which must remain arbiter. In this situation, where two kinds of statutory agency confront the Department, it would be inequitable and make for inefficiency if the presented case were less forcibly put by the smaller unit, namely, the local authority. But in fact there is no reason to suppose that the local authority does get short shrift. The discretionary proposals involving capital outlay which fall within the ambience of a local authority are for day care and residential care units offering a variety of structured supports to mentally disordered people within the community. These discretionary schemes are vetted by the Department in exactly the same way as are projects for hospital building and restructuring. But in all these functions the Department is able to assess competing schemes and competing methods within one national framework. It is difficult to see how individual regional authorities could effectively and acceptably take over that job from it.

In summary, therefore, the involvement of the local authority with the mentally disordered is part of its generic commitment and does not require a structure identical with that of the health service itself. The concept of mental health in the community, to be meaningful at all, depends upon a close, concerned, and sophisticated interaction between politico-social planning at the central or local government level and the various therapies which clinicians can contribute. The range of these therapies, and the circumstances in which they can be made available, must be for the professional to state, not a regional authority; the same goes for the matching provision made within the community and so far as general oversight and control of these local operations is concerned there is very little room for anything useful above the local level save at the central level itself.

A COMPARATIVE CASE: PROVISION FOR THE YOUNG FAMILY

Both in provision for the homeless and in provision for the mentally disordered there has been, *prima facie*, special reason to explore the possible significance of a regional structure, but in neither case are the arguments strong enough to support the regional devolutionists' case. Let us now turn for comparison to another field of work – the care of families with young children, as mandated to local authorities under the Children Act 1948 and Children and Young Persons Act 1963, which is wholly localised in its emphasis.

The function of the personal social services is to redistribute community resources in the favour of disadvantaged families. In practical terms, this commitment is carried out by achieving concrete improvements in the environmental conditions of families – in the direct interests of the children concerned. The same social services must also be structured to avert the possibility of breakdown in the family structure, and to strengthen the personal relationships existing between children and parents.

The agencies concerned, whether statutory or voluntary,

have to act selectively. And they cannot stick rigidly to general rules, if only because there is no clear yardstick by which to measure the personal or environmental difficulties to which individual families are subject. Pre-eminent among these difficulties are low income, restricted earning capacity, stressful housing conditions and ambivalent attitudes to children.

Moreover, members of families are under no *obligation* to look for support from anyone. They can remain indefinitely sequestered unless they identify themselves to one of the supportive agencies, or are brought to notice by a third party. Yet non-accidental injury to children in their own homes, for example, is now widely regarded both as an offence committed by parents and as an indication of default on the part of agencies with powers to intervene. The crucial statutory requirement of local authorities is set out in Section I (1) of the Children and Young Persons Act 1963. It reads:

> It shall be the duty of every local authority to make available such advice, guidance and assistance as may promote the welfare of children by diminishing the need to receive children into or keep them in care under the Children Act, 1948 . . . or to bring children before a juvenile court; and any provision made by a local authority under this subsection may, if the local authority think fit, include provision for giving assistance in kind or, in exceptional circumstances, in cash.

Would a larger administrative structure rectify anomalies and improve the judgement of statutory agencies in deploying scarce resources? The evidence suggests a negative answer. Reliance has to be placed on the quality of judgement exercised by local authority officers at the point of their meeting with a family, and a long line of communication would inhibit an effective reaction to need.

Tangible provision made available under a local authority's powers include:

Arrears of rent/rates.
Payment of arrears, including reconnection charges for gas and electricity supply.
Payment of arrears of hire purchase.

Rehabilitation payments for furniture, furnishings, bedding, removal expenses, etc.
Payments to relatives and neighbours to care for children.
Emergency payments/vouchers for food.
Holidays for parents and children, including transport costs.
Miscellaneous payments for clothing, fares, etc.
Rent guarantees.

But when an authority acts in any one of these ways the material aid it offers must be part of a coherent programme of support which is intended continuously to lessen, not increase, the dependence of the family. A knowledge of local lore is really as crucial as adherence to some centrally stated principle.

It is not clear where a regional level of government would usefully come into all this. For the reasons indicated, if it took over any of the local authorities' functions it would be unlikely to perform them so responsively. If it took over the supervisory, resource-sharing functions of the central government the latter would be effectively stripped of all real capacity to support its essential national responsibilities in this field.

CONCLUSION

It is possible now to recapitulate some at least of the arguments set out in this chapter. The personal social services are the epitome of social care. They incorporate an overt resolution within a society that regard shall be paid to a minority group – perhaps 15–20 per cent of the population overall – who at the adult level have available to them strictly limited life-choices. The restrictions which exist on their choices mean, in effect, that it is probable they will turn at some time or another to social agencies, whether statutory or voluntary. These social agencies, making provision in a variety of ways, are accountable in the last analysis to society itself.

Here tensions multiply. Realistically, personal social services only exist to be curbed: that is, to work themselves out of business. But they will not in fact do so for a long time – if ever. And so long as they exist they must be monitored. Some responsibility must necessarily be accepted by central government. But in practice it can only exercise that responsibility by working with and through the social services authorities themselves. As Rudolf Klein and Phoebe Hall have pointed out, central government's evaluations of professional care-deliverers have got somehow to go along with the latter in their work.[11] Richard Bourne indeed suggests further that it is now deliberate policy on the part of central government not to develop monitoring processes independently of the organisations monitored.[12] Instead the attitude, at least as regards the personal social services, is to help the local authorities to monitor themselves – against the background of national perceptions and criteria but also local insights.

For it is only at that local level that a clear picture can be seen, and effective account can be taken, of the needs and possibilities that arise at the interface between personal social service work and the work of the Supplementary Benefits Commission, the health service and other agencies. And of course this is even more true of the relationship with other departments of local government; a fusion of interest within the same authority is not difficult to compass either by deliberate application of corporate planning techniques or by simple inter-committee policy making. Where the local government structures vary between first tier and second tier, e.g. between counties having social services responsibility and districts having housing responsibility, local agreements consonant with statute must be hammered out, in, for example, provision for the homeless, and these agreements are encouraged by government circulars. There is a natural cross-fertilisation between social services and education authorities and for the time being some overlap, notably in the matter of education welfare functions which in some areas of the country result in specific appointments within the education service. None of these deliberate adjustments which social services committees make within the whole context of local authority planning and practice would be more naturally or more effectively carried out by a form of regional government of the kind proposed in the Memorandum of Dissent, and nor would the limited supervision or resource-sharing functions of central government.

That there is negligible value for the personal social services in purely consultative and co-ordinating councils at regional level has already been argued earlier in this chapter. Relationships with the health service have also been considered – *à propos* specifically the mentally ill and the mentally handicapped; the regional element in health service provision does not create any pressing requirement that the personal social services should be organised *pari passu.* Finally, we also look at the practice of income support – i.e. the payment of minimal cash allowances to persons above the age of 16 years unable to support themselves or their dependants by full-time work, or from their national insurance and pension entitlements. These cash payments are currently channelled through offices whose geographical areas cross local boundaries; but they do not lend themselves to regional arrangements, either. Admittedly the basic statutory cash benefit is not in fact of equal value in all parts of the country, but some flexibility is introduced by the variable rent (or mortgage interest) allowances payable by the Commission, and it could if desired be made for other local cost-of-living differences. But formal delegation of the power to make decisions about the rate of benefit itself would directly offend political canons about proper administration of a national system of support. The regional structure which does already exist within the Supplementary Benefits Commission is a matter of internal management organisation, is not significant for policy-making, and has nothing to do with devolution of power.

NOTES AND REFERENCES

1 Department of Health and Social Security, *Forward Planning of Local Authority Social Services: Capital Projects,* Circular LASSL (74) 22 (HMSO, 1974).
2 *Public Expenditure to 1978–9,* Cmnd. 5879 (HMSO, 1975).
3 *Report of the Committee on Local Authority and Allied Personal Social Services* (Seebohm Committee), Cmnd. 3703 (HMSO, 1968) para. 111.
4 Ibid., para. 582.
5 *Kilbrandon Report,* Appendix D, paras 96–8.
6 E. Wistrich, *Local Government Reorganization: The First Years of Camden* (London Borough of Camden, 1972).
7 Unpublished DHSS/DoE homelessness statistics.
8 London Borough of Camden, *Report to Housing Committee and Social Services Committee,* July 1974.
9 Department of the Environment and Department of Health and Social Security, *Homelessness,* DHSS Circular 4/74 (HMSO, 1974).

10 J. Greve, D. Page and S. Greve, *Homelessness in London* (Scottish Academic Press, 1971) p. 267.
11 R. Klein and P. Hall, *Caring for Quality in the Caring Services*, Doughty Street Paper no. 2 (Centre for Studies in Social Policy, 1974).
12 R. Bourne, 'Why not inspect?', *New Society* (5 Dec 1974).

5 Regional Devolution and Local Government

DEREK SENIOR

Regional devolution, as I understand it, does not mean the reconstruction of the United Kingdom as a federation or confederation of separate states, each with its defined field of sovereignty; nor does it mean the decentralisation by central government of the conduct of some of its present business to region-based outposts of Whitehall. It means the transfer by central government of some of the decision-making responsibilities now exercised by Whitehall, its regional directorates and its *ad hoc* regional agencies, to a level of democratic self-government intermediate in *scale* between central and local government as now constituted, but so similar in *principle* to local government that it could eventually serve as the upper tier of an adequately reformed system of local administration.

What we are here concerned with, then, is regional *government*: not a collection of advisory councils or joint co-ordinating committees answerable to their constituent local authorities, or even a set of elected assemblies serving as the paid agents of central government, but a series of regional *authorities*, directly accountable to regional electorates, having a general concern (and competence to act) for the well-being of their regional communities and executive powers appropriate to their scale of operation

In other words, we are discussing the applicaton to England of some variant of Scheme B in the Government's consultative paper.[1] The variant I prefer would differ from Scheme B in that the regional authorities might not necessarily take over all the functions of all the existing regional outposts of central government, or the governmental functions of all the *ad hoc* regional agencies. It would also allow local authorities to retain direct contact with the Departments of Education, and of Health and Social Security in respect of their service-running (as distinct from development) functions. But it would retain such essential features of Scheme B as a discretionary power for the regional authorities to translate national policies into action programmes adapted to their regions' special needs, a residual power to secure the good government of their regions' people (subject to national protection of their civil rights) and an autonomous financial base.

It was an equally essential feature of Scheme B as originally propounded in the Memorandum of Dissent that the regional authorities should be directly elected. Local authorities as such were not to have 'direct representation in the intermediate level governments', as the consultative paper misleadingly puts it, but only a minority representation on their functional committees on a par with suitably qualified co-opted persons. On the other hand, the assurance that 'there would be no change in the functions of local authorities' was only a politic feature of the scheme, not an essential one – not even, indeed, a logically defensible one.[2] Whether or not it should be adopted initially is a matter of expediency. Ultimately the purposes for which regional authorities are needed will, in my view, require that they should not only draw some decision-making functions down from central government, but also that they should draw up from local government those of its functions which have been conferred upon it only because no more appropriate democratic instrument yet exists. But it may well be legislatively more convenient to leave these functions with the county councils until the time is ripe for a second bite at the cherry, involving a further reorganization of local government itself.

The assumption that we are concerned only with a real devolution of decision-making powers to regional authorities with independent political bases and sources of finance is implicit in the title of this chapter. For if 'devolution' were to mean no more than the formalisation of existing arrangements for co-operation between local planning authorities (as in Scheme G) or the absorption by such reconstituted 'standing conferences' of the present regional economic planning councils (as in Scheme F), its impact on the scope and effectiveness of local government would be negligible.[3]

Having no executive powers of their own and no control over the executive actions of their constituent local authorities, the advisory bodies suggested in these latter schemes could not even produce strategic plans conceived in the interests of each region as a whole; they could only 'co-ordinate', or trim and gum together, the plans conceived by their several constituent county councils in the sectional interests of their artificially segregated populations. If they were ever to be so imprudent as to seek to do more than this, the county councils concerned would simply reject their advice, as Kent rejected the one positive proposal (for the large-scale expansion of Ashford) to emerge from the Standing Conference on London and South East Regional Planning. Central government, for its part, would treat their advice as it now treats that of the regional economic planning councils – as the rival claims of competing regional pressure-groups, all of which can be ignored since all cannot be satisfied. There might be some gain in the field of information, if such advisory bodies employed adequate research staffs of their own and publicised their findings; but it would be only an academic gain. Indeed, in so far as the creation of such bodies deprived the central government of its present justification for setting up joint strategic planning teams, the end result would be a net diminution of the influence of regional needs and potentialities on local authority planning.

Enough has been said, in the Memorandum of Dissent, about the strength of the case for the only kind of devolution that is relevant to the theme of this chapter. It is, however, necessary to say something about the nature of that case, for upon it depends the scope of the functions which the regional authorities should discharge, and hence the character and extent of their impact on local government.

THE CASE FOR REGIONAL SELF-GOVERNMENT

The case rests in part – but only in part – on the evidence accumulated by the Kilbrandon Commission of the public's tendency to view the operation of our system of government with mounting dissatisfaction, if not disaffection; and on the findings – sadly misinterpreted by the majority of the Commission's members – of the 'attitudes survey' it commissioned from the Government Social Survey.[4] This showed that about three-quarters of the people questioned felt strongly that our rulers were not sufficiently informative about what they were up to, or sufficiently concerned to inform themselves about, and respond to, the problems, needs and wishes of ordinary people. But since it also showed that at least the same proportion felt that the situation would not be improved if we had more ordinary people 'running things', it was quite fallaciously inferred in the research report that the remedy for our manifest discontents must lie not so much in institutional changes designed to spread political power, as in persuading our civil servants to be more communicative, receptive and considerate; and the majority of the Commission's members uncritically accepted this conclusion.

A very different interpretation would surely have emerged if as much weight had been given to other no less emphatic attitudes revealed by the survey: for example, that even more prevalent than this 'felt lack of communication' is the feeling that 'the needs of the people in the region would be looked after much better' if the English *regions*, as well as Scotland and Wales, 'had more say in running their own affairs'. (Incidentally, popular interest in devolution was found to be stronger in all parts of England, except the South East, than in Wales, and almost as strong as in Scotland: even the sense of regional identity was found to be almost as strong in England outside the South East as in Scotland and Wales.)[5]

Even if the lack of communication (in both directions) had been the only (or outstandingly) felt grievance in England, it would have been naive to conclude, as the majority of Commissioners concluded, that its remedy required no institutional change, but only a change of heart and a more understanding approach on the part of all concerned, and particularly of public officials. As Lord Crowther-Hunt and his fellow-dissenter observed,

> It is not in the nature of governments and their bureaucracies to provide the people with more information than institutional and other pressures can prise out of them. Nor can we expect governments to seek out, listen to, and be responsive to, the wishes of the people unless the people and their representatives have the institutional power to require this sort of conduct from their rulers. If any believe that the 'communication gap' can be bridged

> by exhortation alone, and without institutional change, then they show a touching faith in the natural behaviour of governments which flies in the face of all historical and contemporary evidence.[6]

This is not, as it might seem, a swipe at our civil servants: it is a comment on the nature of governments, national or local or (for that matter) regional, and on the limitations of our own system of government in particular. In that system there are only two places where governmental decisions can be informed by a comprehensive view of, and concern for, the general well-being of the people affected, and not merely by a departmentally blinkered interest in the adequacy and efficiency of a specialised public service. One is the remote fastness of the Cabinet Room, where the people's needs and wishes can be considered only in terms of a highly generalised national interest, and the other is the local council's policy committee, whose responsiveness is circumscribed by financial dependence, divisive boundaries and a limited discretion within a narrow functional range.

Most of the public decisions that most affect most people's lives are taken by the servants of single-minded ministries and *ad hoc* boards who, with the best will in the world, simply *cannot* be sufficiently informed about, let alone respond to, the diverse and changing ways in which social, economic and environmental problems arise, interact and combine to affect each individual regional or sub-regional community.

What, then, is the basic cause of the discontents identified by the Commission's attitude survey – of the sense of being kept in the dark, of suffering from decisions taken by people who don't understand or won't respond to our needs and wishes, and of being unable to do anything about it? It is not that we are dissatisfied with the way national policies are determined and national priorities fixed: if we are, we have our remedy in a general election. What irks us is the way national policies and priority decisions are implemented in our own areas – the way the executive decisions which actually affect us are made. And what makes these decisions irksome is not merely, or even mainly, that they are taken bureaucratically and at a needlessly remote level, but that they are taken by people who see only particular functional aspects of our community life instead of by people whose business it is to look at the whole picture and decide how best to implement national policies and priorities for our benefit in the light of this synoptic view of our needs, problems and aspirations. However able and however well-informed within their specialised fields the present decision-takers may be, the resultant effect of their unrelated decisions on the regional community is almost inevitably a galling misuse of some of the resources available to it, which is all the more galling because the only avenue of complaint lies up through the local MP to the responsible minister and down from him through the hierarchy of his civil servants or appointees.

In order that our system of government should be satisfyingly democratic, then, it is not enough that all the decisions that palpably affect our lives should be taken by people who are effectively responsible to elected bodies. It is also necessary that such decision-taking should be horizontally organised across the functional board at the lowest level that is consistent both with functional efficiency and with an adequate range of functions at each level, so that the members of each elected body may be as accessible as possible to the people whose lives their decisions affect and may exercise a real control over the way their area's resources are used in the light of a comprehensive knowledge of its needs. It is also necessary that the area with which each elected body deals should be a coherent socio-geographic entity, so that its needs may in fact be comprehensible.

It was not to be expected that any large proportion of the people questioned in the Kilbrandon Commission's attitudes survey should have thus analysed the causes of their discontents and identified the kind of institutional change to which the analysis pointed. (That was what the Commission itself was set up to do, and what most of its members signally failed to do.) It would not have been surprising if their sense of helpless mistreatment at the hands of uninformative, uncomprehending and insensitive administrators should have expressed itself in a demand for a chance to 'run things' themselves. Remarkably, however, this was not what the great majority felt they needed (except in their immediate neighbourhoods). What they did feel they needed was that more say in running their own affairs should be given to 'the region': they felt that their needs would be better looked after if more things were run for them by representatives whom they had elected and could get at, and whose level of operation was no more remote than it had to be to enable them to tackle effectively the problems of their own regional community. They felt, with a sure political instinct, that it was only by filling this gap in our system of self-government through representative bodies with a general responsibility for the welfare of their electorates that the 'communications gap' could also be closed.

THE FUNCTION OF REGIONAL AUTHORITIES

The principles on which the case for regional self-government rests do not of themselves determine either the scale on which it should operate or the scope of the functions it should exercise. Of course, elective decision-making bodies should operate as close to the people whose lives their decisions affect as may be consistent with functional effectiveness and a wide field of concern, and this principle applies to the allocation of functions between regional and local government as well as between central and regional government – or, for that matter, between the EEC and central government. It does not, however, follow that the scope of regional government should be confined to matters which are not now decided either in Whitehall or in County Hall. The fact that it has been found impossible to handle satisfactorily a wide range of governmental problems except at an intermediate level, and that the *ad hoc* agencies and outposts of central government set up to handle them at this level operate independently of one another in the same region – these are indeed major elements in the case for the creation of regional authorities; and there is a strong presumption that, when regional authorities are created, they should in the first instance have transferred to them all the functions that now have to be handled in this way. But there may well be other functions which have been entrusted to (or not yet removed from) local government, not because local government as now organised is competent to perform them, but only because the elective regional authorities that would be competent to handle them do not exist. Just as our accession to the EEC not only subjected us to international control in some spheres which had previously been unregulated, but also entailed the transfer of some decision-making powers from our central government to the EEC, so also the introduction into our domestic system of government of a regional component must be expected ultimately to entail the transfer to it of some functions now formally conferred upon, but not adequately discharged by, local government, as well as some areas of decision-making that are still concentrated in Whitehall but could with advantage to all concerned be devolved upon region-based authorities.

How far the scope of regional government should extend at the lower end of its range must therefore depend on how much local government is structurally competent to do with an acceptable degree of functional effectiveness. Under the 1972 Local Government Act, local government in England has been quite deliberately made structurally competent to do a great deal less than it could have done under the city-region scheme so cogently advocated by the Ministry of Housing and Local Government in its written evidence to the Redcliffe-Maud Commission[7] (and adopted for Scotland, with the exception of that quaint anachronism, the Kingdom of Fife), or even under the previous government's partial improvement on the Redcliffe-Maud proposals.[8] In particular, local government in England has deliberately been made structurally incompetent to run a unified health service. The first Green Paper on this subject, issued by the Ministry of Health while the Redcliffe-Maud Commission was sitting, contemplated the unification of the NHS within local government if that Commission's recommendations resulted in an appropriate framework of some forty city-region authorities;[9] but since the 1972 Local Government Act created an entirely inappropriate framework, the government which passed it left itself with no choice but to unify the NHS outside local government, and thereby to put the health and welfare aspects of the community care needed by millions of hapless people not only under different authorities, but under radically different kinds of authority. Similarly, local government in England has been made structurally incompetent to run a unified water service. In Scotland the creation (by the same government) of suitable regional authorities has enabled water supply, sewerage and river purification functions to be transferred to them from the *ad hoc* appointed boards by which these functions had previously been separately exercised. But in England the government deliberately left itself no choice but to transfer local government's remaining water supply and sewage disposal functions, together with the water-related functions previously transferred from local authorities to river boards, to newly created *ad hoc* regional water authorities. And the statutory duties it laid upon these authorities will inevitably cause them to insist that future urban development follows the directions that will maximise the cost-effectiveness of their own services, regardless of the manifold considerations that regional authorities would balance against that factor. Long-planned and much-needed developments have already been killed by their refusal to give any priority to the necessary water and sewerage installations.

Nor is this all. Local government in England had deliberately been made structurally incompetent to handle satisfactorily the functions still nominally left to it in the field of urban planning and development, especially in the growth-generating areas where the problems involved are most acute and intractable. As the authors of the 1972 Act observed in the White Paper which adumbrated its provisions, 'none of these proposed metropolitan counties can practically contain the solutions of all the planning problems of the conurbations'. They did, indeed, go on to express their expectation that 'where it is impossible to meet all housing and redevelopment needs within the county boundaries, the answer will lie in development well outside the metropolitan area, in accordance with a carefully worked out regional plan'.[10] But as Lady Sharp scornfully commented,

> This is what we have been trying these last ten or fifteen years. There have been carefully worked out regional plans, but they have not been acceptable to the outer county councils or to the outer district councils – quite understandably so . . . if we cannot face the idea of a local government structure for these metropolitan counties that will include both the urban and the rural areas, and so enable them to solve their vast problems of redevelopment, of traffic, of transport for themselves, we may have to look for something in the shape of provincial councils to do the planning and also have the powers to see that the plans are carried through.[11]

In the event, predictably, the 'carefully worked out regional plan' for the North West proposes no development 'well outside the metropolitan areas' but concentrates almost all its development proposals in the remaining open spaces within the boundaries of the metropolitan counties – or conurbation counties, as they might more honestly be called.[12]

It was, in fact, never intended that structure planning should be entrusted to the sort of county (metropolitan or shire) that has emerged from the 1972 Act. This function was created in the 1968 Planning Act (and suspended for the time being) in anticipation of a reform of local government based on the structurally plannable entities which, as the responsible ministry told the Redcliffe-Maud Commission in set terms, are absolutely indispensable for this purpose. 'Structure' in this context, as the Development Plans Manual explains, means 'the social, economic and physical systems of an area, including its transportation system';[13] to be structurally plannable, therefore, an area must comprise whole social, economic and physical systems – as a handful of shire counties coincidentally do, but every metropolitan or conurbation county is expressly designed not to do. There is, indeed, statutory provision for the submission of joint structure plans for the parts of adjoining counties that together constitute a coherent sub-region or city region, just as there was provision in the 1947 Planning Act for the creation of united planning districts; but the prospect of county councils thus subordinating their sectional interests to the interest of the sub-region as a whole is about as likely in the one case as it proved in the other. The joint structure plans on which some inter-county teams are now working can be legally invalidated by the withdrawal of any one of the sponsoring counties at any time before they are approved by the Secretary of State. In these circumstances structure planning has become virtually a non-function – a mere obstacle in the way of the production of operative local plans. There is increasing pressure for its replacement in the short run by a simple, quickly formulated statement of policy guidelines; in the longer run it seems likely to give way to the kind of district plan that can serve as a basis for the comprehensive acquisition of development land.

But who, then, is to be responsible for translating broad strategic decisions (such as the accommodation of three-quarters of a million more people in the general vicinity of Reading, Aldershot and Basingstoke) into plans for the functional structuring of such urban regions as integrated wholes? This is a task that cannot be simply neglected without disastrous consequences, so if regional authorities are created it will automatically fall into their laps. With it, of course, must go the powers required to put these plans into practical effect. To quote again from the same speech by Lady Sharp: 'If there is one thing that we have learned over the past years it is that it is useless to have planning powers in one authority and the powers to implement the plans in another. This gets you nowhere'. Or as Sir Robert Grieve once put it, 'Planning that does not bear on development is mere doodling'.[14]

Given the scope, thus supplemented, of the functions already exercised by intermediate-level governmental agencies of one sort and another, it is evident that the central concern of regional government should be the economic, social and physical *development* of the region as a whole for the benefit of the regional community as a whole, including the making and continuous remaking of strategic plans, together with such control over local planning as may be necessary to make it conform; the programming of capital investment in infrastructural facilites of every kind that are of regional importance; the location of employment within the region; the assembly, servicing and disposal of land for urban development and the execution of key projects (such as the creation of new towns and villages) essential to the timely implementation of strategic plans. Some non-developmental functions, closely bound up with such aspects of development as transportation and traffic control, should also be included: a not inconsiderable benefit of the introduction of regional government, for example, would be the re-establishment of democratic control over the police service on a scale appropriate to its operational needs.

It should be noted that in Scotland the new regional units of local government are so defined that most of their authorities will be quite competent to exercise, for themselves and on behalf of weaker neighbours, most of the functions for which regional authorities are needed in England and Wales. This, together with the claim of cultural nationalism, makes the case for a different *form* of devolution to Scotland as a whole (if not also to Wales as a whole) quite consistent with the view that the English regions are entitled to the same *degree* of devolution in the general sphere of economic, social and physical development. It should also be noted that the word 'function' is here used not as a synonym for 'service' (e.g., health, housing, education, planning) but to denote an area of decision-making, which may cover only a part or aspect of the historically accidental collection of activities which we have grown accustomed to regard as 'a service' (e.g., the development of hospital and consultant services and medical research, but not the running of district hospitals, health centres and community health services). Broadly speaking, regional government in England would be responsible for community *development* through a variety of agencies, including local government and its own executive arms, while local government would be primarily responsible for community *care* – making the best use of existing facilities in direct dealings with the citizen. The necessary 'interlocking' between the two levels in particular services would, in my view, be better secured through a continuous cyclical process – local initiatives arising from locally ascertained differences and changes in local need would inform and influence regional policy guidelines for local plans which would be subject to regional approval of their investment implications – rather than through the subordination of local to regional authorities, tempered by representation of the former on the latter.

REGIONAL GOVERNMENT FINANCE

A similar relationship would subsist between regional and central government. At the same time, each level of government, local, regional and national, would have its own sphere of exclusive responsibility, its own sources of revenue and its own general competence to act (within appropriate constitutional safeguards for the protection of individual liberties) for the benefit of the community it served. Given the broad division of responsibilities suggested above, it would seem most appropriate that local government should be financed by the rates, and regional government by the values accruing from the comprehensive acquisition of development land at existing-use value and its disposal (when serviced) for development in accordance with a planning brief at market value, together with private motoring taxation.

It is not possible to give any meaningful estimate of the likely yield of these two possible sources of regional revenue, since their effective rates must vary widely with economic circumstances, with regional development policies and with the energy policies of our own and other governments. But taking the current existing-use value of undeveloped agricultural land as about £700 an acre, the annual rate of its development as 40,000 acres and the market value of land with permission for its least valuable urban use as £26,000, the betterment yield from new development alone would be over £1000 million a year. Against this must be set the cost of servicing the land for development, but this is balanced by a corresponding relief of the burden on rates, water rates and sewerage precepts. Then, taking the rate at which our four million acres of urbanised land are redeveloped as one per cent a year, a comparable yield would accrue – unless, as the Community Land Bill's Explanatory Memorandum would seem to assume, urban land were to be predominantly redeveloped for less valuable uses.

The yield of taxation on private motoring (non-commercial motor vehicle duty, petrol tax and driving licence fee) now varies from Budget to Budget, and even between Budgets, according to the balance-of-payments situation as well as to the Exchequer's revenue requirements. But when North Sea oil meets all our needs, the rate of petrol tax will presumably become once more determinable by purely fiscal considerations. If this source of revenue were transferred to regional government, the rate of petrol tax would also have to be variable from region to region, for it is essential to the financial autonomy and responsibility of regional government that it should have the same freedom as local government enjoys (if that is the right word) to fix the rate at which it levies its own taxation. Merely to determine how the resources made available to it should be allocated between its functions is not enough to make a democratic authority financially responsible: it must also be accountable to its electorate for the scale of its total expenditure and must accept the onus of presenting the bulk of the bill.

The inter-regional variation would not, of course, need to be very wide, for the yield at any given rate would vary with the amount of motor traffic, which in turn would largely determine how much would need to be spent on the regional authority's development functions. It need never be so wide that it persuaded more than an infinitesimal proportion of motorists to drive across regional boundaries to fill up their tanks, assuming that these boundaries were drawn, as they obviously should be, along the sparsely populated 'traffic watersheds' between regional centres.[15] (It is, of course, the fact that local authority boundaries are not drawn on this principle – or, indeed, on any other – that rules out the possibility of allowing *local* government to levy petrol tax at differential rates.) The only substantial part of a regional authority's expenditure that would not be roughly proportionate to the needs arising from automobility is the cost of modernising the older inner-city areas. It is in the regions that have the heaviest liabilities in this respect that the buoyancy of motor taxation revenue will be sustained the longest, because their levels of car ownership have furthest to rise to saturation point; but in the meanwhile their greater needs will call for supplementary funds from central government.

The allocation of national resources *between* regions (which Whitehall miscalls regional planning) is, of course, an essential part of the national planning which only central government can do, and will remain a necessary function of central government even if regional planning proper – the allocation *within* regions of whatever resources are available to them – is entirely devolved to elective regional authorities. Fiscal and financial devices that discriminate between regions, such as regional employment premiums, regionally selective employment taxes, loans, grants and tax reliefs for industrial development in declining regions, are all legitimate tools of national policy for the correction of inter-regional economic imbalance, in order that under-used resources may be more fully employed without overheating the economy elsewhere. An equally legitimate tool would be the supplementation by central government of local or regional authorities' revenues where taxable capacity is low in relation to public service and investment needs – provided it were used only in these areas and for this purpose. It ceases to be legitimate only when (as in the case of the present rate support grant) it is used also to make good a chronic and ubiquitous discrepancy between the cost of what sub-national authorities are required by Parliament to do and the potential yield of the sources of revenue they are allowed to tap. Used only for its proper purpose, and not to palliate revolt against the Treasury's craving to monopolise sources of revenue or to give Whitehall a pretext for meddling in matters too local for it to grasp, the rate support grant would contribute only a fraction of its present 66 per cent to local government resources; and since no region would be so predominantly impoverished as many local government areas, a regional equalisation grant should constitute a still smaller proportion of total regional resources – certainly not enough to compromise regional government's financial responsibility.

By the same token, it is and must remain a proper function of central government to determine in the national interest such things as the location of international airports, the planning of the national motorway network and the inter-regional distribution of such nationally important enterprises as aluminium smelters. But only the absence of regional authorities can justify central government's use of negative controls over the location of industrial and office employment – ostensibly to alleviate *inter*-regional imbalances but effectually to dictate the *intra*-regional distribution of urban growth. Planning control is meaningless when a senior colleague of the minister to whom a would-be industrial developer is appealing has already promised him his choice of locations in one region in return for taking part of his development to another. It would be difficult enough for a planning authority to make any sort of sense of the pattern of human settlement and transportation in its area if nothing more than the provision of such basic infrastructural services as water supply and sewerage were in the hands of a functionally blinkered *ad hoc* authority intent only on its statutory duty to balance its sectional books; it becomes quite impossible if a department of state with an equally exclusive field of concern virtually decides where within a region people may work.

Besides the levelling up of the resources available to the poorer regional or local authorities whose own tax revenues would at any given time be deficient in relation to their needs, there are two purposes for which central government could legitimately provide *all* regional or local authorities with some additional income from national funds. One is to stimulate the initial development of new services and facilities, or extensions of existing services, which Parliament has decided are desirable everywhere in the national interest, but which need to be provided as integral parts of regional or local development programmes at a cost which would initially be burdensome to an authority with particular geographic or demographic characteristics. Recent examples are regional parks (which, to serve effectively as counter-magnets to our national park wildernesses, need to be measurable in square miles rather than acres) and nursery schools. But such pump-priming inducement grants should be available only for limited periods, and should not be either so generous or so numerous at any given time that their availability, rather than a balanced assessment of regional or local needs, tends to determine the shape of regional or local development programmes.

The remaining purpose for which a contribution from national funds may be warranted is to justify the retention by central government of a reserve capacity to enforce the maintenance of *minimum* standards in a service. Complete regional or local autonomy in the setting of priorities might theoretically result in the lowering of the standard of one service in one area to a level which public opinion, expressed through Parliament, regarded as a national disgrace. It is highly improbable, of course, that local and regional opinion, expressed through directly elected parish (or neighbourhood), local and regional councils, would fail to demand the correction of any such lapse more quickly, more vociferously and more effectively than could any national lobby; but the possibility would exist and should be catered for – provided the means to that end can be adequately hedged about with safeguards against their abuse. For it must be emphasised that we are here concerned with nothing more than that limited degree of central government participation in the financing of local and regional government functions which is strictly necessary to justify the retention by central government of default powers to secure the provision of nationally demanded services at the lowest tolerable standard. This does *not* mean that central government's contribution should be on such a scale as to serve as a pretext for any claim on its part to a right to impose *uniform* standards.

THE MYTH OF NATIONAL UNIFORMITY

It is often argued by opponents of regional devolution that the people of this small island set a higher value on uniformity of standards, which any worthwhile measure of regional devolution must put at risk, than on the adjustment of priorities between services to regional needs which it would make possible. Nearly always it is the education service that is cited in support of this view. But the argument is fallacious, even in this specialised context, on two grounds. First, *national* uniformity is desired only in those educational provisions (such as grants for university students)which should always have been, and should continue after regional devolution to be, the direct responsibility of central government, because they are inherently unsuitable for administration at a lower level. Elsewhere the demand is for *regional* uniformity: parents in Portsmouth might indeed get angry if they found that the standards of public education in Petersfield were higher, but not one in a thousand of them would know *or care* whether they were higher or lower in Peterborough, Peterlee, Peebles, Pwllheli or Penzance. Secondly, the argument takes it for granted that as matters stand, with central government either administering our services through appointees or controlling their administration by local authorities through the power of the purse, we do now have uniformity of standards, or at least a close and ever closer approximation to that presumptive ideal. But nothing could be further from the truth, as survey after survey has revealed.

Even in our hierarchical National Health Service, as Sir George Godber testifies in his chapter, there are still, after a quarter of a century, great disparities between one region and another. Such improvement as has taken place in hospital development he attributes to the fact that the planning of it has been a regional exercise, and a regional organisation is at last beginning to correct one of its worst features – the maldistribution of junior hospital staff. It is only in Scotland and Wales, with their independent advocacy of further funds, and to a lesser extent in the North East, because of the energy of its regional organisation, that any great progress towards levelling up has been made; in the North Midlands, where facilities were at first nearly as bad as in South Wales, there has been no such improvement because there has been no independent political influence exerted on the region's behalf. Sir George adds that in the present set-up no *redistribution* of resources between the better and worse provided regions of England is practicable. The DHSS just dare not provoke the protests that would ensue. It cannot begin to make good the glaring regional deficiencies until substantial *additional* funds are made available to it; and the prospect of their being made available, on anything like the scale required at any time in the foreseeable future, is about as remote as the possibility that, if they were made available on that scale, they would be used solely for that purpose.

As Sir George also testifies, the outcome of stronger regional institutions with some financial independence 'could be that some areas in the country will show the way by better provision and make it incumbent on others to follow'.[16] And indeed all experience of the effect of bringing democratic political pressure to bear *at the right level* justifies the conviction that if the development of the NHS had been entrusted to elective regional authorities of the right scale and geographical composition at any time in the last quarter of a century, its standards would now be much more *uniformly* high throughout Great Britain. Even those senior members of the medical profession who are most fearful of contamination by contact with the democratic process are beginning to realise that dependence on the Treasury has been insulating them not from competition with other services for scarce resources but from the backing of their potential patients' representatives.

Some opponents of regional devolution claim, as David Eversley has done earlier in this book, that the country would not tolerate regional variations even in the social and environmental standards applied by governmental authorities, and therefore that any institutional change that would allow such variations is as much a non-starter as legislative devolution. If, they argue, it is inconceivable that there should be a NHS in some regions but not in others, as would be possible under legislative devolution, then 'logically'(!) it is equally inconceivable that regional variations should be permitted in such matters of taste or social judgement as the preservation of Georgian buildings or the maintenance of Parker Morris housing standards. This contention is equally invalid, and on the same two grounds: we do, in fact, tolerate many such variations quite happily, and could tolerate many more with advantage to our regional communities and no damage to our national unity; and the implicit assumption – that such variations are now prevented by the centralised taking of those decisions which under executive devolution would be taken by regional authorities – is false.

In areas of urgent housing need local planning authorities do quite freely, and with the hearty approval of all concerned, seek to hasten completions by permitting the erection of houses that fall much further below Parker Morris standards than would be allowed elsewhere; and in cities with vast slum clearance problems, whatever the law may say, the medical officer of health has always, in my experience, very sensibly delayed representing houses as unfit until his local authority was ready to demolish and replace them. Again, while it is of course right that central government should concern itself with the preservation of our national heritage of good Georgian domestic architecture, it is also right that undistinguished specimens of indifferent aesthetic quality or historic interest should be preserved at a higher opportunity cost in a region which has no other examples of the period, and few even of these, than in one which is stiff with them. And in the latter case only the Georgian Society would think of objecting if a regional authority had, and exercised, the power to decide that such a building should not be allowed to stand in the way of a much-needed public development.

CENTRAL GOVERNMENT RESPONSIBILITIES

The three types of subvention from central government outlined above need not and should not together amount to a great deal by comparison with the independent revenues which local and regional government would together derive from rates, development values and non-commercial motor taxation, and therefore would not materially detract from the necessary financial independence and responsibility of local and regional authorities. Central government would retain executive and financial responsibility for major development projects of national or inter-regional significance, and for those parts of each service (such as Sir George Godber identifies in the health service) which by their nature need to be provided by one authority for the whole country; but it would be relieved of the greater part of its present liability for rate support and of other substantial burdens in the fields of health, housing and urban development. By and large, its savings would balance the revenues it lost, while the transferred revenues would enable local and regional authorities between them to maintain the provision of existing services, with such slight improvement of their standards as might be derived from such economies as the elimination of multi-district areas from the health service and the eventual halving of the number of planning authorities (see below).

Central government would also, of course, remain responsible for controlling the overall amount of public capital investment (which in turn governs current expenditure in subsequent years), but it would do so by means of a block allocation to each region for the next instalment of its rolling development programme. The process of allocation should not, of course, proceed by separating out a regional programme's functional elements, reassembling these with the corresponding elements of other regions' programmes into departmental packages, thrashing out national priorities between departments, trimming the departmental packages accordingly, breaking each trimmed package down into regional elements and then leaving each regional authority to recombine its sanctioned elements as best it could into a comprehensive, but consequentially distorted and disjointed, development programme. In addition, central government would need to satisfy itself that the regional programmes, collectively, represented a feasible balance of demand on available sectoral resources; but it would not first decide how these resources should be allocated between departmental programmes at national level and then apportion bits and pieces of these programmes to individual regional authorities. The initiative in formulating development programmes reflecting regional priorities would lie with the regional authorities. Their proposals to spend more on one service and less on another than national policy indicated would generally cancel one another out, but the overall outcome would sometimes be a different balance between, say, school-building and housing than the relative forcefulness of the responsible ministers would otherwise have secured. When that happened the Cabinet would have cause, and ought, to question whether its own Olympian view of the best interest of the nation in this respect was likely to be as valid as that of the elected regional authorities. If, on the other hand, the combined effect of the regional programmes proved inconsistent with a national interest or constraint of such a nature that only the central government could form a valid judgement of it, the programmes should be modified accordingly. In either case the process of validation and adjustment could be properly organised only on a cyclical basis, and it is one of the real advantages of interposing a limited number of elective development authorities between central and local government that it makes practicable the kind of dialogue between levels that such a process requires.

THE CASES AGAINST REGIONAL DEVOLUTION

The concept of regional devolution outlined above is assailed by its critics (notably David Eversley and A. R. Isserlis in this book) from diametrically opposite directions. David Eversley maintains that so long as even the most major and essentially national decisions on economic development (such as where North Sea oil should be brought ashore) rest with central government, these decisions will so pre-determine all lesser decisions (as to the location of employment within regions and the scale and mix of their industrial development) that there will be virtually nothing left for regional authorities to decide, no matter how extensive may be the range of their nominal decision-making powers. A. R. Isserlis, by contrast, contends that unless central government retains ultimate control over the making of even the most minor and essentially local decisions in every departmental field, there will be virtually nothing in these fields that it will continue to be capable of doing.

Eversley's thesis seems to be that if regional devolution stops short of separation – the transfer of legislative sovereignty – it cannot be anything but a meaningless sham, not worth the trouble it involves. That the framework within which regional authorities would be free to take executive decisions would itself be centrally determined is enough, in his view, to nullify the value of that freedom – which is at least as good an argument for abolishing local government as for not instituting regional government. He can find no scope, in the field of environmental planning, for any change that would empower a regional authority to take *final* decisions, to become the *final* instance of appeal, and without such finality, he asserts, devolution has no real meaning. Yet the final decision in classes of planning appeal that together make up 75 per cent of all cases is taken by an inspector, and it would surely be better if in these cases he reported a recommendation to the regional authority responsible for strategic planning for its final decision, as in other cases he reports to the Secretary of State for his. True, the Secretary of State could, with Parliament's consent, revoke the Statutory Instrument that confers this power of final decision-making on inspectors. Is it then argued that even if the making of all executive decisions in all fields of domestic policy were devolved upon regional authorities, such devolution would still be a meaningless sham simply because Parliament could at any time repeal the statute by which they were established? Does the argument, in the last analysis, amount to anything more than the truism that executive devolution involves no transfer of sovereignty?

Isserlis differentiates between legislative and executive devolution and has no difficulty in demolishing any case for the former – though in my view he overstates the extent to which the same law in practice has the same effect in all parts of the country. In actual fact it would not make one iota of difference to what happens now in Snowdonia and the Highlands if a Welsh Assembly were empowered to pass a law denying *standard* improvement grants to English residents and a Scottish Assembly could prohibit strip-tease shows. Differential enforcement of the law has the same effect as a different law. His opposition to executive devolution, however, is based on a more serious misconception. His thesis is that central government could not effectively exercise its responsibilities for preparing legislation, monitoring its implementation, approving strategies and otherwise securing the execution of national policies in each departmental field if its departments did not themselves 'possess executive functions of the kind that would empower and equip them to do, or know, or answer for anything tangible relating to any particular part of the area of government business concerned'.[17] But this assumes that they *can* properly achieve the purposes of national policies now, when they are thus empowered and equipped.

Surely the whole *raison d'être* of executive devolution is the increasingly evident and resented fact that, no matter how much detailed executive power and experience in using it they may have, departmental heads in Whitehall and the departmental civil servants responsible to them, wherever based, do not, and in the nature of things *cannot,* with the best will in the world, know *how* national policies can best be collectively implemented in the widely varying and constantly changing circumstances of each region. And it is therefore an essential ingredient of executive devolution to regional authorities that the responsibility of central government for securing the execution of national policies should thereafter be confined to those projects and those elements in the public services which by their nature need to be tackled at national level. Within this range central government would continue to be endowed with all the necessary resources and detailed executive powers, would acquire the same depth of experience and maintain the same capability as before; but the regional authorities would assume the responsibility and raise the finance for securing the execution of those remaining elements in national policies which by their nature need to be concerted across the functional board at regional level and adapted to differing regional conditions. There is nothing quaint about the proposition that, since Whitehall does not *and cannot* have the degree of contact that would enable it adequately to understand the regional implications of its broad national policies, it should simply be relieved of any need to do so, and that the working out of these policies in terms of executive action in the regional context should be left to authorities whose members and officers would be in continuous contact with what their regions were needing and feeling.

This would in no way prejudice the continuance of effective national government in matters which really were of essentially national concern. But it would, of course, mean that things of essentially regional concern would be done in different ways and on a dfferent scale in different parts of the country. To enable this to happen is the whole object of the exercise. Westminster politicians and Whitehall civil servants would indeed find it hard to accept at first: that, no doubt, is why the relevant questions in the Government's discussion document were designed to suggest their own answers. But they would not find the consequences so unacceptable.

There is no warrant whatever for David Eversley's assumption that a regional authority would be more inclined than central government has been to neglect the social and environmental needs of the older urban areas. It would be free to do so, of course, as central government now is; but that is not in itself a reason to suppose that it would do so. Representing as it would (even in the North West) a cross-section of the national community from inner city through affluent suburb, stockbroker belt, industrial and market towns to villages and open country, it would be financially and territorially equipped, as local government is not, to deal with the problem by making the dispersal of people and jobs from inner urban areas to new towns beyond the green belt serve its ulterior purpose of enabling decent living conditions to be provided for the people who need or want to go on living in the inner urban areas. It is, indeed, precisely the extent to which regional devolution would facilitate and induce the only effective solution of this problem, coupled with the manifest futility of central goverment's tinkering attempts to atone for having deliberately made local government structurally incapable of tackling it, that puts such a strange complexion on opposition to regional devolution in anyone who cares about the plight of the inner urban areas.

In fairness to A. R. Isserlis, he does recognise that many of the economic, social, physical and technological elements in the problems of government policy are grouped into broadly recognisable regional patterns; that the regions defined by the spheres of influence of main centres are necessary frameworks for considering issues that transcend local government boundaries; and that it is useful to consider many other matters in a regional dimension But he believes that these acknowledged functional needs can be met by a much fuller and more seriously purposeful decentralisation of the exercise by central government of its present decision-making powers.

This was the solution I advocated in Volume II of the Redcliffe-Maud Report as a necessary complement to the reform of local government on a city-region basis, given that central government was then patently unwilling even to consider the alternative of executive devolution.[18] But to serve its purpose it would have to be accompanied not only by a quite radical reorganisation of central government itself, enabling the region-based civil servants of all departments to be effectively responsible to a political decision-maker

(Minister of State) in each region, instead of to their departmental heads in Whitehall but also, in present circumstances, by a large extension of central government's planning and executive activities into the no-man's-land which local government has been made incompetent to occupy. These consequential changes would, in my view, require far more 'political and administrative will-power' (Mr Isserlis's words)[19] than those involved in regional devolution, while the prospects of adequately meeting the functional needs in view would be far less certain and the mounting demand for regional democracy would not be met at all. It is not where the ultimate decision-makers sit that is important to regional feeling, as Mr Isserlies himself implies; but neither is it only what they decide; it is also to whom they are accountable. The administrative decentralists have still to demonstrate the feasibility, the implications, the acceptability and the comparative effectiveness of their alternative solution.

THE GEOGRAPHY OF REGIONAL UNITS

I now come to the question of the scale and geographic composition of the units of regional government in England, given the functional scope indicated above. This seems to me a matter of paramount importance, and I am utterly dumbfounded by the perfunctory attention given to it by the Kilbrandon Commission. Its majority, having decided that the English regions should at least have councils with advisory and co-ordinating powers, assumed without question that the eight areas defined by central government for the purpose of decentralising the conduct of its own economic planning business would automatically serve their own radically different purpose well enough. It confessedly did so for no better reason than that the majority of the Redcliffe-Maud Commission, having teetered on the brink of giving its provincial councils executive functions but failed to make up its mind on this crucial issue, had adopted these eight units (with two substantial modifications) for want of any rational basis for doing otherwise; and it did not even bother to investigate the case for these modifications.[20]

Even the dissentient minority did little better. Having plumped for elective regional authorities with a high degree of autonomy, they simply adopted the five 'provinces' which I had defined, in my Memorandum of Dissent from the

Redcliffe-Maud Report, solely for the decentralised exercise of central government functions and expressly on the assumptions that there was to be no devolution whatever from central government and that the top tier of local government was to consist of city-region authorities with structurally plannable areas. I went on to point out that the alternative assumption (of a willingness on the part of central government to devolve the making of governmental decisions on all matters needing to be tackled at an intermediate level) would call for the replacement of both my city-region authorities and my five 'provinces' with about fourteen regional authorities with areas formed by the combination of major with adjoining minor city regions.[21]

Lord Crowther-Hunt and Professor Peacock explained their extraordinary decision 'purely on "management" grounds', without even a side-glance at the cardinal necessity for elective bodies to represent real and coherent communities. Admittedly they did so 'on the assumption that the new county and district boundaries make sense in planning terms' – evidently without realising the enormity of this assumption – and added that 'if they are ill-designed for this, as many people believe, then clearly different considerations would arise': but these they failed to specify.[22]

The dissenters did take account of the need (since water management must be a function of regional government) for the boundaries of the regional authorities to be closely related to physical watersheds.[23] It has always been taken for granted by the responsible government department that, in England, hydrological areas must always be unsuitable for self-government on the ground that they bear little or no relation to the patterns of settlement and social activity with which multi-purpose democratic authorities are mainly concerned; and this is generally true at the local government level. But, at the scale appropriate to regional government, it is the reverse of the truth in all parts of England except the Midlands, where any boundary separating the West and East Midlands from each other and from the regions based on Bristol and Leeds would require the same sort of special arrangement as now has to be made between the Welsh and adjoining English *ad hoc* water authorities. Elsewhere it can be demonstrated, as the dissenters indicate, that complete river basins can be put together to form regional units (up to fifteen for England and Wales) that can hardly be faulted from the standpoint of social geography. To put it the other way round, regional units *of this scale,* defined in terms of socio-geographic coherence and community of interest in respect of the activities and problems with which regional government should be concerned, can have boundaries at least as close to physical watersheds as those of the new Scottish regional authorities; and these, as the Government itself has acknowledged by transferring all water-related functions to them, have boundaries that are hydrologically quite acceptable – except in the case of that egregious anachronism, the Kingdom of Fife.

It would, of course, as the dissenters suggest, be possible to group these fifteen units into five – but only at the cost of a serious loss (unacceptable where *elective* authorities are in question) of cohesiveness and sense of regional identity. (For example, as the South West Regional Economic Planning Council has pointed out, the Plymouth-based half of its area is entirely distinct from the Bristol-based half in almost every relevant respect: its problems, indeed, are diametrically different, and in so far as its people look beyond Plymouth for specialised facilities and services they look not to Bristol but to London.) Moreover, there would be no compensating gain in functional effectiveness in any of the fields appropriate to regional government; in some, indeed, there would be a palpable loss. And even the claim – feeble as it is – that five regional units would make more 'managerial sense' than fifteen in relation to forty-six first-tier and 364 second-tier authorities falls to the ground unless it is assumed that these local authorities will long continue in being after the regional authorities have been created. But is it reasonble to suppose that they can?

IMPLICATIONS FOR LOCAL GOVERNMENT

As was suggested at the beginning of this chapter, it may well be politically expedient to endow the new regional authorities in the first instance only with powers now exercised by *ad hoc* boards and outposts of central government; but once they are established it surely cannot be long before we are constrained to transfer to them those more exacting functions in the fields of land assembly and structural planning, transportation, urban development, infrastructural investment programming and the like (not to mention such related incidentals as the police and fire services, regional parks and so on) which they will be manifestly more capable of discharging effectively than administrative counties whose areas in all but half a dozen cases correspond more closely with the settlement pattern of the Middle Ages than of the motor age. And when that time comes it will surely be equally obvious that we really have no need for two layers of local *administration* below the regional level – that there would, indeed, be everything to be said for abolishing the metropolitan counties and replacing both the shire counties and their districts with district authorities of the intermediate scale of the new health districts – the only units at any local level whose areas have been defined, in part at least, by reference to functional requirements and the facts of social geography.

Such district units, unlike the great majority of new local government districts, would indeed make sense in local planning terms (staffwise as well as areawise); they would be of the right composition and scale in relation to their areas' needs for the running of all the personal services; not least importantly, they would reunite under one democratic authority the health and social welfare services which millions of people simultaneously need. It would then be possible to eliminate that fifth wheel on the NHS coach, the multi-district area helath authority, which exists only to paper over the administrative chasm between the NHS and the county social service departments, but which serves to obstruct communication between the two functionally necessary levels of health service organisation and to hinder the operational unification of the NHS at what has always been recognised as the only level at which operational unification is possible – the district.

It may not be too fanciful to see as a further advantage of such a change that it would assuage all the resentment caused by the recent reorganisation of first-tier local government by making it possible for the counties to revert to their historic boundaries; for it is to the traditional geographic counties and all the activities associated with them, not to the administrative counties, that county loyalties attach – loyalties which existed for a thousand years before the counties administered anything but justice, and which are nowhere stronger than in Lancashire, where an administrative county has never contained as much as half of the county population, and in Yorkshire, which has never been an administrative county. The Post Office may yet have to reverse its current alterations of postal addresses – alterations which were rightly considered needless when Greater London was carved out of the Home Counties.

Yet another advantage of such a change is that it would meet in practice the case put forward in the Redcliffe-Maud Report, and widely accepted among the members of urban authorities, for the unitary principle. Though the suggested larger districts would not be strictly unitary in the sense of being the only sub-national democratic authorities operating in their areas for all purposes, they would in fact be the only democratic authorities with which the citizens of their areas would have to deal and their scope would span both the personal-service and the environmental groups of functions; they would, indeed, be at least as 'unitary' as the authorities actually proposed in the Redcliffe-Maud Report.

One final point must be heavily emphasised. Since it is presumed that in the first instance the proposed regional authorities would deal only with matters not now within the local government field, and that when they do eventually take over functions from local government it will obviously be necessary for the existing administrative counties and districts to be superseded, there is no earthly reason why the boundaries of the new regional authorities should be defined in terms of the boundaries of these existing local authorities. On the contrary, there are reasons of overwhelming strength why we should not thus perpetuate some of the worst aspects of the structure we shall be discarding. Specifically, any amalgamation of existing administrative county areas will not allow the formation of either hydrologically acceptable regional units, or planning entities that do not sever substantial parts of major existing and potential city regions from their centres, or health regions that do not cut off whole health districts and parts of several others from their most accessible centres of specialist hospital facilities, consultant organisation and medical retraining services – as the map of present regional health authority areas all too clearly shows. If a lack of coincidence between the boundaries of regional and county authorities would make it too difficult for the regions to assume some of the functions proposed for them by the Kilbrandon dissenters, such as the approval of county structure plans, it would be far better to leave these functions for the time being in the hands of central government. There are limits, I submit, to the values and benefits that we should be prepared to go on indefinitely sacrificing on the altar of administrative convenience.

NOTES AND REFERENCES

1 *Devolution within the United Kingdom: Some Alternatives for Discussion* (HMSO, 1974) paras 20–7. A description of all the Kilbrandon Commission's schemes for regional government (termed Schemes A–G) appeared in this document, and are reproduced in the appendix to this book.
2 Ibid., para. 24.
3 See appendix, pp.
4 Royal Commission on the Constitution, *Devolution and Other Aspects of Government: An Attitudes Survey*, Research Paper 7 (HMSO, 1973).
5 *Memorandum of Dissent*, paras 46, 51, 62 and 65.
6 Ibid., para. 80.
7 Royal Commission on Local Government in England, *Written Evidence of the Ministry of Housing and Local Government* (HMSO, 1967) pp. 60–6.
8 Department of the Environment, *Reform of Local Government in England*, Cmnd. 4276 (HMSO, 1970).
9 Department of Health and Social Security, *National Health Service: The Administrative Structure of the Medical and Related Sciences in England and Wales* (HMSO, 1968).
10 Department of the Environment, *Local Government in England: Government Proposals for Re-organisation*, Cmnd. 4584 (HMSO, 1971) para. 32.
11 *Hansard, House of Lords*, vol. 316, no. 78, col. 1125.
12 *The Strategic Plan for the North West* (HMSO, 1974).
13 Department of the Environment, *Development Plans: A Manual on Form and Content* (HMSO, 1970) paras 3–6.
14 Personal communication.
15 *Traffic in Towns: Report of the Steering Group* (HMSO, 1963) para. 46.
16 Sir George Godber, Regional Devolution and the National Health Service, p. 78.
17 A. R. Isserlis, Regional Devolution and National Government, p. 179.
18 *Report of the Royal Commission on Local Government in England*, Cmnd. 4040–1, vol. II (HMSO, 1969) paras 474–93 (Redcliffe-Maud Report).
19 Isserlis, Regional Devolution, p. 188.
20 *Kilbrandon Report*, para. 1191.
21 *Report of the Royal Commission on Local Government in England*, Cmnd. 4040–1, vol. II, paras 493–501.
22 *Memorandum of Dissent*, para. 325.
23 Ibid., para. 323.

6 Regional Devolution and National Government

A. R. ISSERLIS

Earlier contributors to this book have commented on the case for regional devolution by reference to particular major fields of national government responsibility. This chapter looks at some of the implications for the national government process generally – and sees them rather differently from the way in which they are seen by Derek Senior in his chapter.

THE REGIONAL IDEA

In Britain, the region is nowadays accepted as an increasingly useful dimension between the national and the local for perceiving some of society's trends, wants, opportunities and constraints, and relating them to the business and the options of government. It is of course only one dimension among many that are needed. It is not by any means the most significant. For some purposes it is not even relevant. But it does undoubtedly have a value. As a matter of plain fact, the people of Britain do live and work and have their being within a complex layer-upon-layer structure of economic and social and cultural communities of interest of which some (though only some) are conveniently definable in regional terms. There are of course many different ways of defining regions, none of them entirely satisfactory for all purposes.[1] But the important thing is that a dimension between the national and the local is agreed to exist.

All this is already well recognised in the study and teaching of human geography and in other social science disciplines. It manifests itself in economic and environmental planning. It is reflected in the organisation of most publicly-run services and utilities. It is taken into account to a growing extent in the collection and presentation of governmental statistics – perhaps indeed at the price of insufficient attention to equally important units of measurement of other kinds.[2] In short, regionalism has come to stay.

Today's debate on regional devolution, however, is about taking the regional idea a great deal further. What is now at issue is the extent to which, in future, the region should be used not merely as a dimension for perception and administration, but also as a justification and a means for limiting or even fragmenting the actual power of the national government.

Regions are of course already used as a convenient basis on which to divide up some of the government's work-load and organisation into more easily handleable and locally accessible units. They are likewise already being used in some parts of the country, though still only to a limited extent, as a framework for planning and co-ordination in an attempt to remedy some of the consequences of a continuing failure to relate the pattern of local government organisation to its socio-geographical context.[3] In the case of Scotland and Wales, of course, these uses of the regional dimension have been developed especially strongly, and given greater effectiveness and visibility, through the government's now long-standing practice of maintaining very considerable regional offices in Edinburgh and Cardiff, linked to very small Scottish and Welsh Offices in London and headed by secretaries of state statutorily responsible as regards their respective regions for many of the functions that would otherwise be exercised by their ministerial colleagues.

But all this is still only administrative decentralisation, and not devolution. Even Scottish legislation is only law made for Scotland – and closely similar to that made for the rest of Britain – by Parliament at Westminster. Even the separateness of the Scottish legal system is relatively superficial, and continues only to the extent that the Westminster Parliament allows it to do so. Not until recent years has there been any serious hearing, accompanied by any serious possibility of success, for proposals in Britain to establish real separate regional authorities, endowed with real power, at the expense of the power of the government of the country as a whole. Of course the government of the country as a whole is not usually the main consideration in proposals of this kind. Most of them seem to stem simply from a desire to meet needs claimed to be indentifiable within certain regions, especially Scotland and Wales, from the point of view of those regions' own inhabitants – or at any rate of some influential groups among their voters. The assumption is made that those alleged needs can only or best be satisfied by changes in governmental structure on devolutionist lines. In most cases the effectiveness of the government of Britain as a whole appears to be only of secondary importance in the development of the thinking. Ideas about power to the regions emerge; their national implications are then considered as consequentials; not surprisingly in such circumstances, even the most far-reaching of such implications are then perceived, if perceived at all, as at worst tolerable and at best positively to be welcomed; and they are then prayed in aid of the prior assumption that some kind of regional level of government is desirable.

This is true even of much of the Kilbrandon Report. Admittedly the two authors of the Memorandum of Dissent, Lord Crowther-Hunt and Professor Alan Peacock, based a great deal of their case on what they claimed to be a *pre-existing* need for dismantling some of the existing national government structure – one of them because he evidently didn't like the way in which national government had so far been operating, the other because he apparently didn't like having so much government anyway, and both because they wanted Westminster and Whitehall to concern themselves less with this country and more with Europe and the rest of the world. But even those distinguished dissenters established this somewhat curious intellectual partnership only, it would seem, because they both in their differing ways were anxious to convince themselves and others that there was a significant amount of ineradicable and legitimate desire, within a number of regions in England as well as in Scotland and Wales, not merely for more or better or different kinds of government policies and decisions and administrative styles – and of ways of getting the yields of other people's taxation – but also, and specifically, for some measure of devolution of national powers to new organs of government at regional level.[4]

Predictably, this assumption has also powerfully affected the attitudes of the parliamentary parties. The political offerings now being made, which in the first instance are of devolution to new regional bodies to be set up in Scotland and Wales, seem to be based on the proposition that voters who matter to the parties concerned in those regions do definitely want and therefore ought to be shown *some* measure of devolution, leaving the consequences in terms of the effect on national government to be somehow coped with, come what may.

Yet, in relation to many of the devolution proposals currently under discussion, it may be questioned whether many or any of these effects on national government would in practice have been considered even by those proposing them as being quite so acceptable, let alone attractive, if they had not seemed to be consequentials of meeting regional needs and pressures deemed to be of major importance. And in fact there is a great deal of room for argument, though this chapter is not the place for it, about what those regional needs and pressures really add up to, and whether those inhabitants said to be expressing them are all that numerous and single-minded or can be expected to have really thought them through. For although people live in regions and sometimes have a bit of regional consciousness (or at least will say they have if they are asked), the often conflicting things that in practice they mainly want of their elected masters – e.g., better policies, quicker decisions, smoother methods, more information, higher public expenditure, lower taxation, more interference with other people, less interference with themselves – are usually about matters which are either of a local government kind or of a national government kind. They are very seldom regional things by their inherent nature. In fields of quite different kinds, people's feelings of identification with their regions may indeed be important: a careful attention to regional cultural characteristics no doubt helps commercial television producers, for example, in providing a background for the effective advertising of detergent powders and tinned soup. But when it comes to what people want from government, regionalism is often no more than a convenient and currently fashionable peg on which to hang claims or grievances which could in fact be at least as well aired in some other way.

It may be, of course, that as regards Scotland and Wales, as a matter of practical politics following the successes of nationalist propaganda, a decisive part of the regional case must be regarded as having in fact already, rightly or wrongly, been conceded, leaving little basis for useful continuing argument. But even there some scope must remain for further thought; and there is still more time before final decisions are reached about the regions of England. So there is at least a case for taking a closer look at some of the implications of regional devolution for national government, by reference to the practicalities of the actual tasks and expectations that the national government currently has to face in the future irrespective of whether a regional tier of government is introduced or not.

THE MEANING OF REGIONAL DEVOLUTION IN THE NATIONAL CONTEXT

Certain rather general points need to made at the start. The first is that, although one need not be too apocalyptic about it, devolution on any major scale does mean structural change going well beyond the kind of reform that Britain's system of government has hitherto undergone during this century. It is probably true that in practice, 'given the political will', to use a phrase in the Kilbrandon Report, any of the proposed schemes could in the end be put into effect and made to work – somehow. Life would manage to go on. Yet by the same token there is very little in the history of this or other countries to justify a belief that the introduction of any system of power transfer to sub-national levels, however considerable and cleverly devised, would in practice be successful in counteracting for very long the centralising influences in the political dynamic of a modern society. Through one development or another, mechanisms which seem to assure independence of action to autonomous or semi-autonomous sub-national bodies tend far more often in the event to be eroded, overridden or circumvented (David Eversley has given some examples in his chapter) than to be strengthened in their effectiveness over time; and the process is usually accompanied by tension, friction, frustration, and sometimes outright conflict. This may not by itself be a reason for not seeking devolution if that is what is desired. But it must enter into any assessment of the costs and benefits that devolution would entail. Government is an expensive commodity in terms of resources of many kinds – including human energy and time and tolerance.

Changes which are likely to put a significant extra strain on those resources need all the stronger justification.

And even if that justification is in the event deemed to exist already as regards Scotland and perhaps Wales, simply because of the strength of the demands and expectations that by good or ill management have been allowed to grow there, so there will be all the *greater* need to justify up to the hilt any proposals for change relating to the regions of England. For in the English regions many of the partly factitious kinds of consideration which enter into the debates about Scotland and Wales do not operate anyway. And whereas it is one thing to accept and contain the risk of allowing the effectiveness of Britain's national government to be needlessly damaged by cosmetic surgery on the Celtic extremities, it is quite another and much more serious thing to contemplate unnecessary dissection of the nation's English heartland.[5]

And dissection is what it could be, at any rate if there were devolution of the power to legislate. For the term 'legislative devolution' is in fact a euphemism for enabling the nation-state to be gradually cut into pieces. You start by not letting it be cut into pieces very much. Yet once you have conceded, with whatever paper reservations and safeguards, that on certain matters Westminster's writ shall no longer run, you have thrown away your main defence against demands that it should no longer run on other matters too, and in places beside Scotland and Wales. There will be pressures for the pieces to separate still more. And the countervailing tendencies mentioned earlier will have to operate in conditions of increased stress. Wherever you draw the dividing line now between what law-making is devolved regionally and what is retained nationally, you will find that at some time in the future a need will arise in practice, on some politically important economic or social issue, to consider adjusting or crossing that dividing line in response to new experience. That must mean a possibility of retracting some of the devolution as well as a possibility of extending it. But any proposal for such an adjustment will no longer be automatically capable of relatively calm discussion and settlement within one sovereign legislature. Instead, it will have to be thrashed out between two or more rival authorities, even though one claims to be the major one, amidst a clash of actual or would-be sovereignties. Such a situation may or may not be creative, but it must certainly be tense.[6]

Moreover, any tendency to encourage fragmentation of national government power seems to need specially wary attention at a time when technological and economic and social developments both at home and abroad are at once shrinking this country's effective size and making it more dependent than ever on co-operation with countries overseas. Our relationship with the European Communities is one case in point. Labour and capital, production and marketing, cultural and political co-operation, all require a reduction and not an increase in the number of boundaries and separate jurisdictions. The Memorandum of Dissent rather surprisingly used this aspect in the dynamic of our national and international situation as an argument not merely for improving the general efficiency of our governmental system but also, and specifically, for breaking it up very considerably by means of regional devolution of executive functions. It seems at least reasonable, however, to take the contrary view: that the probability of continuing growth in the extent of Britain's exposure to international influences and obligations will call not for less but for more integrated direction and management of the country's public business, if the national government is to be in a position effectively to assess the country's needs and potentialities, make the most of what it can get to match them, and deliver what it promises in return. This argues for caution about devolution not only at the legislative but also at the executive level.

Indeed there is a sense in which the customary categories for considering and differentiating various possible degrees of devolution – legislative, executive, and merely administrative – are rather unreal. In national government in practice the three functions are not entirely divisible. However, there can be some value in looking at them separately up to a point.

THE IMPLICATIONS OF LEGISLATIVE DEVOLUTION

The legislative is of course the fundamental part of any government machinery, since it is about the promulgation, enforcement and observance of the law as a regulator of relationships among individuals and between citizens and society. So one must expect very important implications for the role and effectiveness of national government to flow from any system of regional devolution that gives regional authorities independent legislative power. To make sense, this legislative power must allow those authorities to decide, in effect, that people's freedom or property or convenience can be encroached on by other individuals or by public agencies for differing reasons of law and not simply of fact, and up to differing limits specified regionally and not nationally, according to the part of the country they happen to be in (over and above the kind of controlled differential encroachment that in Britain is already barely tolerated in the form of varying local taxation burdens).

In the terms in which they are usually presented for discussion by their advocates, the various devolution proposals do not usually appear to go this far. Some of them do of course talk about devolution of legislative functions; but they do so rather in phraseology which implies that what is under discussion is merely a region's freedom of choice of how best to deploy public resources for the public good. What was not brought out very clearly in the Kilbrandon Report, for example, and has hardly been brought out at all in the official discussion documents that followed it, is the fact that legislative devolution, if it is to have any real meaning, must mean much more than that: it must really be about fragmenting the law, and not simply making it. Thus is must also mean the possibility that people themselves, and not merely their public authorities, will have to suffer different law in different parts of the country. Derek Senior in his chapter makes light of this point, on the ground that national law already varies from place to place in the way in which it operates, because general powers are used in different ways by different local authorities.[7] But those local authority powers are prescribed nationally; the degree of discretion permissible in their exercise is nationally limited; their operation is, ultimately, nationally controllable; and the national legislature can if necessary take them away. Devolution of national legislative powers to regional authorities, if it is not to be a fraud, is not about discretionary local administration of that kind, but about power to vary the thrust of the law itself. And that could mean variations in our societal framework going well beyond what most proponents of devolution usually seem to be thinking about.

In town and country planning, for example, legislative devolution could mean each separate regional authority's not just overseeing the implementation of local plans but also making its own rules as to the rationale on which people's land can be taken, or their freedom of activity interfered with, or their privacy from their neighbours eroded; and for what planning law offences people can be sued or sent to prison, and to what extent. In housing it could mean each separate regional authority's defining the circumstances in which a person may be forced to keep his house standing up, or pull it down, or get out of it, or let someone else stay in it, or meet out of his taxes some of the costs of other people's accommodation. In health it could mean regional authorities controlling who may be allowed to practise in the health care professions, and which people may have access to them under what conditions, and whether this or that form of treatment is permissible, and who can lock up whom on the ground that he is mad. In the personal social services it could mean the possibility of regionally different laws governing responsibility for children, support for the elderly, care for the handicapped, the giving or withholding of help in kind to those without means. In education it could mean significant variations among regions in the duties owed by public authorities to students and their parents, and in the powers and obligations of teachers and other professionals. In other social matters it could make it possible for four-letter words to be punished as obscene in one region, but only five-letter words in another; for liquor to be sold to young people of different ages in different parts of the country; for criminals to be hanged on one side of a border but on the other side only flogged. In local authority arrangements it could mean the possibility of variations in practice, in organisation, and in the rights of local citizens as electors and ratepayers, who would have even less recourse than at present to the protection of a national government. And so on. If it does *not* mean the possibility that on matters of these kinds the law could be different from one region to another according to what the regional authority decides, then it can hardly amount to real legislative devolution at all.

Moreover, it should be noted that personal rights and freedoms could be affected not only by the devolution of legislative power *per se.* One of the present important functions of central government is the exercise of a kind of appellate jurisdiction designed to ensure that local authorities and other similar bodies, in making local decisions affecting private rights and property, are not only conforming to national policies accepted by Parliament but are also complying with understood principles of administrative justice. Under at least some of the devolution schemes put forward, that jurisdiction too would have to be devolved; and an individual's appeal against a compulsory purchase notice or a planning restriction or a demolition order or a dismissal from a school's staff could then be decided not in accordance with nationally uniform principles but in the light of the policies and rules laid down by his particular regional authority.

This all means that if the proportion of governmental business selected for legislative devolution were to be on anything like the scale which its proponents usually suggest (and otherwise there would be a little point in the exercise), the national government would cease to have any effective capability not only as regards the planning and control of a large number of essential public services and activities but also as regards the regulation and protection of a wide range of personal and corporate freedoms and opportunities. And such safeguards as an executive or financial veto operated subject to approval by the national Parliament would be too clumsy and politically sensitive for more than rare utility – especially since the loss of legislative and *a fortiori* executive functions in relation to the matters concerned would mean that the national government would be lacking in the responsible experience needed to legitimise such intervention.

Moreover, the effects would in practice go wider than the particular functions concerned. Most, though not all, of the proponents of legislative devolution appear to accept that such matters for example as industrial policy, communications policy, and fiscal and economic management generally, would have to be left with the national government. But – as Dr Eversley brings out very clearly in his chapter on environmental planning – the effectiveness of government in this field is in countless ways dependent on its having the power and the experience to ensure the necessary co-ordination and consequential action, at all levels including the legislative, within many other fields as well. Industrial location control must be geared with control over town and country planning. National communication networks must intermesh with local networks. Control over local authority expenditure and money-raising must be related to national policies on spending and taxing and borrowing generally. And so on. Legislative devolution in relation to any one sizeable part of this complex structure of interrelated responsibilities would make the whole structure much less operationally viable. Thus even when people advocate legislative devolution to regions in respect only of a clearly delimited range of governmental functions, they are in fact also seeking, whether they realise it or not, to hamper the effective exercise of most of those other functions that are to be left with the national government.

THE IMPLICATIONS OF OTHER KINDS OF DEVOLUTION

But at least those who propose legislative devolution are recognising reality to some extent: in the fields directly concerned, they would put the legislative power where they would also put the executive responsibility. The less extreme devolutionists – more numerous and more realistic in other ways – tend generally to advocate leaving all effective legislative power at the national level where it is at present, but devolving to regional authorities a considerable range of independent executive responsibility, to be exercised within what is usually described in some such terms as 'a broad framework of prescribed national policies'. And this kind of executive devolution (as distinct from an agency arrangement) is based on two highly questionable assumptions. One is that a national government and Parliament can continue to handle the legislative function effectively if there is no longer at the national level such a degree of executive power and answerability and contact, in relation to the matters concerned, as to provide the continuous experience, understanding and stimulus which the legislative responsibility calls for. The other is that there are meaningful processes called general policy formation, promotion of major objectives, policy-monitoring, strategy approval, and the like, which are capable of independent existence and organisation, and can be effectively carried on and made to stick by national ministers and departments not themselves possessing executive functions of the kind that would empower and equip them to do or know or answer for anything tangible relating to any particular part of the area of government business concerned. These assumptions can certainly not be justified by any evidence from experience.[8]

On the contrary, what experience does make clear is that national government can only secure the implementation of broad national policies, and indeed will in practice only be able to develop the attitudes and the knowledge for even devising such policies, if it also possesses fully, and demonstrates not too seldom, the power (and therefore the necessary prior experience and information) to say Yea yea, Nay nay, to some of the less broad things that the policies are in practice about. Effective policy is what you think about what you actually do or control.

This of course does not mean central departments running all government business in all its detail. For local community affairs the running is done by local authorities. For many other matters there are the specialised public agencies. But these nevertheless operate on the basis that on all essential matters Whitehall and Westminster have a decisive power of ultimate control; there is a context of specific national government responsibility; and therefore there is continuous national government interest and contact. With local authorities it is possible to keep this on an acceptable basis of relationship, involving considerable local discretion in practice, because it is known that, at the crunch, the national government can and often does intervene and exert its powers, and in detail, when it wants to.

In town and country planning, for example, approval of local authorities' broad local strategies can work only because, if necessary, the national government can call development applications in, revoke permissions, decide appeals, withhold loan sanctions, refuse certificates for industrial development. Similarly, the ten-year social service or long-term education plans of the local authorities can be approved and left for local implementation because the national government has the visible whip hand over borrowing and rate support grants and various specific activities – and also ultimately commands legislative power – and can thus intervene if it thinks things are going wrong. A corresponding situation exists in fields like the NHS, and even in the state-owned utilities. This would not be the case if in a number of material respects the national government were deprived, in favour of a new regional tier of government, of having anything but a vague general oversight. A minister's views about local authorities' plans or public agencies' practices would hardly be likely – or be seen by the country or by the Cabinet as likely – to carry very much weight with such bodies if he were bereft of any real controlling power as a result of having had to hand over most of his sticks and carrots to new regional bodies.

One reason for the confusion which many devolutionists seem to display when they propose separating major policy responsibility from executive functions is that they draw a false analogy from the central tutelage over local government. Failing to appreciate that in all essentials Whitehall has never in fact devolved to local authorities any of its own national functions whatever (as distinct from allowing local authorities a degree of discretion in the exercise of their *local* powers), they mistakenly see the existing moderately successful central/local relationship as suggesting the basis of a new kind of relationship, an unholy *ménage à trois*, based on the castration of national government and the interposition of a new regional level of government enjoying much of the national government's former powers. They then confound the confusion further by thinking of this new regional level as taking to itself some of *local* government's powers too.[9]

Derek Senior, indeed, appears to be justifying much of his own kind of advocacy of regional devolution not so much by reference to any case for moving governmental powers from a national to a regional (i.e., non-local) level, as by arguments designed to show that the existing reorganised local government pattern is wrong; that there should be regional as well as sub-regional local authorities; and that given such regional local authorities, with some functions that might then be transferred to them from what are now separate public agencies, there could be more freedom for local government generally from national government control. In other words, he is arguing less for regional devolution from the centre than for regional reorganisation of local government spiced up with a wider range of functions and a bit of increased freedom from Whitehall. There may be something to be said for this. But it is not primarily about regional devolution of major functions and powers from national government, which is what is currently being debated.

The failure among devolutionists to perceive the realities of how governmental power operates in practice is most clearly illustrated by the way in which the Memorandum of

Dissent, although it shrinks from proposing legislative devolution, recommends a very substantial actual transfer of executive powers, going well beyond mere agency arrangement, to regional governments both in Scotland and Wales and in regions of England. According to the Memorandum, the result – indeed, one of the main aims – will be to restrict ministers and officials of the national government, and by the same token the members of the national Parliament, to 'major policy making in a European context' – but in such a way as to enable them to 'ensure that the Governments of Scotland, Wales and the English regions are giving proper effect to Common Market and United Kingdom policies.'[10]

Exactly how they are to do this, however, is something of a mystery. Policy, whether major or minor, needs information to make it relevant, experience to make it sensible, and power to make it stick. But the national government according to the devolutionists would be very limited in its information, for it would be deprived of its own regional offices, denied direct access to local authorities, and indeed discouraged from knowing British domestic affairs in any detail at all. And so would its national Parliamentary watch-dogs: in order 'to participate in policy making in the meaningful way demanded by a mature democracy' they are apparently to 'shed some of their present day-to-day errand-running on behalf of their constituents – e.g., investigating Mrs Snooks' complaint',[11] because they ought to be looking outwards at Europe, instead. In short, as regards knowing anything about Mrs Snooks and her fifty million individual fellow citizens, the national government's intelligence will apparently have to consist of however much or however little by way of information and perception is fed to it by those very regional authorities over which it is supposed to be exercising supervision in the interests of national policy. Poor Mrs Snooks.

As for experience, the national government is evidently not going to be allowed by the devolutionists to have much of that, either. In relation to all the wide range of governmental functions concerned, it will clearly cease to have any sizeable corpus of staff trained and skilled in the actual exercise of accountable decision-making or even monitoring: such staff will have to be split up among the regional authorities, and any skeletal residuum retained as a kind of inspectorate at national level will have to operate without the essential ingredient of continuous personal contact with those exercising executive functions. Their task will be all the more difficult because among the executive functions proposed to be transferred to the regions are some which are of a highly specialised advisory and scrutinising nature, dependent for their exercise on the availability (rooted within the overall executive structure) of scarce personnel with high qualifications and substantial experience in very particular fields – radiation hazards, medical research, high-grade structural engineering, specialised company law, and so on. Under the devolutionists' proposals the national pool of such expertise will have been broken up.

But this will be only a part of a much larger administrative consequence of executive devolution: the breaking up of the civil service generally. Recruitment, training, interchangeability, *esprit de corps*, and virtually all other factors entering into the effective management both of the quality and the quantity of governmental manpower, will all suffer from the degree of fragmentation proposed. And this in spite of the new requirement which the Memorandum of Dissent, for example, would seek to lay on the national government, that its departments should act as a resource for professional and expert staff to advise new and more powerful committees of the House of Commons as part of a scheme of major policy-making which 'dovetails into the new demands of the Common Market dimension'.[12]

And power to give the major policy-making any real meaning? As argued earlier, policy does not mean much if it is not accompanied by the ability to say, and say effectively: Yea; Nay; or Sorry, no cash. Yet under the devolutionists' proposals there will be very few opportunities for the national government ever to exert the realities of power in this way, once a species of horse-trading from time to time has fixed an inter-regional allocation of non-differentiated public expenditure. How then are national government ministers to give or withhold approvals to regional plans on any basis that really matters? How are they in fact to 'ensure' that regional authorities are giving proper effect to national policies? How, indeed, is a minister to carry much weight at all, either in the country or in Cabinet, if his executive functions and his control over spending are for practical purposes no longer there?

One is left not only feeling very sorry for Mrs Snooks the

individual citizen – who is apparently to be no longer a prime concern either of the national government or of the national Parliament – but also a little concerned for quite a few of the national government's ministers. Theirs will be a curiously thin and lonely life: brooding like impotent overlords; introducing legislation on other people's business; promulgating policies they cannot enforce; and generally trying to keep up a fiction that they matter. For they will not be allowed, in the functional fields concerned, actually to do things which do matter: spending money or saving it, agreeing to a proposal or refusing it, stopping something or letting something go on. Their role will be solely that of having a general view, planning a strategy, looking ahead – things which, without executive functions as well, are interesting topics for academics but not real tasks for politicians responsible to an electorate.[13]

The Memorandum of Dissent contains also a curious extra twist to this failure to understand the nature of power. Presumably in order to compensate for the lack of clarity about what it is that the newly created regional authorities and the newly castrated national government, respectively, will actually do, it speaks of 'ordinances' to be issued by the regional bodies, but approved by the national government, 'to promote the good government and general welfare of the people'.[14] Outside the decorative but antiquated statutory preamble which is still used to describe certain petty policing powers of local authorities, such language in a prospectus offered to the whole British public can hardly have been paralleled since the days of the South Sea Bubble. It cannot be too strongly emphasised that good government and general welfare are terms which have no meaning unless expressed and procured in specific terms. If the regional ordinances contemplated are merely for minor local adjustments of general codes, like town by-laws about dogs and ditches, barbers' shops and bassoons, then they are not significant anyway. If they are for anything more than this, then they are regional legislation, and the proposal is really for devolution of legislative powers about important functional matters, subject to a veto – which has already been discussed earlier in this chapter.

THE POWER OF THE PURSE

But in any event legislative power, executive power and administrative power are at the end of the day dependent on one thing that underpins them all – finance. If it is not to be a mere frustrating farce, devolution as distinct from mere agency arrangements or from decentralisation must make a significant change in who decides how much should be taken from which private pockets for what public purposes, and where.

And it is here that can arise the kind of fragmentation of policy and decision-making that is most difficult of all to square with the object of ensuring continuance of effective national government in matters of essentially national concern. This is of course well understood by the extremists who advocate virtual independence for Scotland and Wales in the belief that they can finance it by swingeing taxes on offshore oil extractors; pirates have always preached local autonomy when it supports the hope of exclusive rights to rob those who trade in their nearby seas.[15] But devolutionists of a more moderate kind cannot side-step the problem in quite that way, and they have not come forward with convincing proposals for supporting real regional powers of decision-making with real regional powers of spending that would not seriously weaken what they profess to accept as necessary — an effective national capacity as regards the general scale and direction of functional policies, the equitable allocation of national resources, and the overall management of the national economy. Switching existing taxes from national to local control is no answer, and nor is bringing in new taxes specially for local use.[16] An independent regional taxing power, if it were to produce any revenue worth raising, would in the interests of national economic and fiscal management have to be controlled or offset by the national government in exact proportion to its apparent regional utility. And as regards expenditure, an inter-regional allocation of block spending power would have to be accompanied by devices influencing the way in which that spending power was used, if broad national functional policies were to be anything more than pious national political aspirations. Nor is there in fact any evidence or prospect that individual citizens in any sizeable number in any part of Britain would for long, in practice, accept very material differences between themselves and their fellow citizens in other regions as regards either the methods and scale on which they are taxed or the broad priorities on which the proceeds of such taxes are spent. For these as well as for a number of more detailed reasons one must remain very sceptical about all the financial panaceas which accompany the various schemes of devolution discussed nowadays. Even the Kilbrandon Report itself, which is relatively realistic on finance, has to fall back on the proposition that '*Given the political will*, we think the scheme could be made to work' – which begs rather a lot of questions.[17]

AN ALTERNATIVE APPLICATION OF THE REGIONAL IDEA

But none of this is to suggest that the national government cannot do with *some* reform on regional lines. The arguments in this chapter are against the fragmentation and transfer of national government power. They do not dispose of the case for improvement in the way in which that power is used. And if one examines the situation from that point of view, it becomes possible to make more practical use of some of the evidence and arguments put forward by those who favour devolution.

Theoretically, one alternative to regional devolution on this approach would be an agency arrangement under which regional authorities exercised some of the national government's powers and functions as conditionally trusted agents. However, it is difficult to see how this could operate in practice without a degree of frustration developing which would defeat the object of the exercise. It is of the essence of a regional authority as envisaged by devolutionists that it should represent and be accountable to a regional electorate and possess a genuine independence of action on at least some of the matters which are at present within the control of the national government. An arrangement which offered only a limited and withdrawable discretion still under the national government's control would be unlikely to work to the satisfaction either of regional or of national interests and aspirations. There is no really acceptable half-way house between devolving power and retaining it.

But when one looks closely at the devolutionists' general diagnosis, as distinct from their various prescriptions, it is evident that the allocation of power is not in fact the only or perhaps even the main thing that their dissatisfaction with the present system is really about. What they are really principally concerned with is an alleged lack of national government responsiveness to circumstances and needs and feelings in different parts of the country; an alleged inaccessibility and remoteness; and an alleged failure to co-ordinate policy and action across departmental boundaries in a way that takes account of the interlocking nature of public business and its impact in the actual community. Along with this goes a feeling that in its structural organisation the national government is too centralised and unwieldy for policy effectiveness. And at the same time, at least among some devolutionists, there is the contrary feeling that in some ways it is *too* effective, and that diffusion of its presence would reduce its tendency to develop its power still further.

With these elements in the diagnosis one can have a great deal of sympathy. The role, scale and complexity of the national government have been growing immensely for many years, and are still growing today, and it would indeed be surprising if there were not a need for looking afresh at its workings in the respects described. Admittedly some of the criticisms commonly made are exaggerated or misapplied. Government is often accused of remoteness or unresponsiveness when what has really happened is that policies or decisions do not happen to have found favour substantively with the critics concerned. The complaints about lack of co-ordination are sometimes based on sheer ignorance of the extent to which, within the government machine, co-ordination is in fact achieved.[18] The concern about ministerial work-loads is in fact seldom justified except where the ministers concerned are handling their work-loads wrongly anyway. The denigration of government efficiency generally, and equally the fears of governmental imperialism, are among some devolutionists less the result of practical observation than of fixed doctrinaire hostility to Westminster and Whitehall.[19] Nevertheless, there remains a strong case for reforms to make the system more likely to work with greater acceptability and with greater effectiveness, and indeed to achieve greater harmony in the satisfaction of both criteria.

But in order to get less government overall, you do not necessarily have to add anything up to a dozen more governmental authorities to the national one you already have. In order to get better and more co-ordinated government, you do not necessarily have to weaken it by breaking it up and parcelling much of it out to new and autonomous bodies. In order to get more accessible and responsive government, you do not have to interpose a new level of authority between it and the people it serves. Instead, you can reorganise the structure of government itself, so that without any fragmentation of its powers its presence is diffused more widely throughout the country and it is more open to the insights and information that can be derived from fairly direct contact with the community within each region. The unitary national power can remain. Its exercise can as far as possible be put on a regional basis. In short, you can decentralise the national government's presence and administration.

It is important to note that there is no evidence from experience in Britain hitherto to suggest that decentralisation of this kind cannot go a long way towards meeting the needs to which devolutionists point. Until now, the development of regional offices of national government in England, and the measure of co-ordination involved in the setting up of regional economic planning boards and councils, have amounted to little more than a few faltering first steps towards decentralisation on any significant scale.[20] In Scotland and Wales the steps have of course been much more considerable, but there too a great deal more would need to be done before it could be said that decentralisation was being given a really fair trial.

What the experience does already show, however, is that potentially the concept of decentralisation has a great deal to offer, notwithstanding a number of well-known frustrations which seem to have arisen largely because the process has not yet gone far enough.

For that potential to be fully developed, a number of important things would need doing. They would require political and administrative will-power, but much less than would be involved in actual transfer of power from national government to regional authorities. For example, the dispersal of Whitehall staffs to regional offices in England could be undertaken at a much faster pace than hitherto. The staffs concerned and the work they do could go up to a much higher level of executive and policy-advisory responsibility and career expectation than has hitherto generally been the case. Those departments with no real regional presence at the moment – including the Treasury – could be made to provide one. Those which are out of line as regards their regional pattern could as far as practicable be made to conform. The technical modernisation of the governmental machine, so as to facilitate effective information and control across distances, could be speeded up – provided that Parliament modified its generally grudging attitudes towards Civil Service administration costs. The co-ordinative machinery within each region among the various departments' regional offices could, as earlier indicated, be made much more structured and positive than is evident in the present regional economic planning boards – with a stronger official apex to the co-ordinated hierarchy (at present there is usually a lone under secretary with no interdepartmental authority) perhaps backed by a peripatetic or periodically resident minister charged by his colleagues to keep them in touch politically with the needs and feelings of the region as a whole.[21] The ministers and Whitehall managements of the departments to which these numerically and operationally stronger regional officials would still belong could entrust them with the maximum of discretion consistent with national ministerial accountability. The result would be that, in virtually all fields of government having a territorial significance, more of them could do more of the kinds of things, at high level as well as low, that are at present done on behalf of ministers by officials sitting in London.

Nor need the process of adjustment stop there – where indeed it already nearly is in Scotland and Wales. Some of the other developments which devolutionists are after could also be incorporated into this kind of decentralisation. Block regional allocations of public expenditure, for example, however difficult under any arrangement, would at least in a decentralisation scheme be fraught with less uncontrollable risk of inequity and of getting the national sums wrong. There would still be such problems as the conflict between functional and territorial priorities, and the difference between national and regional perspectives, but there would be a framework of common unitary power in which to sort them out. And within that framework the things decided and done for or to a region would be likely, because more of them were being done *in* the region, to accord more closely with the facts of life in the region and the perceptions and aspirations of the regional people themselves.

This links up with the other question, of giving people in each region more of a feeling that they are somehow consulted *as* people of that region, and have some kind of say in policies or decisions which especially affect the region's affairs. The mere fact that a substantial part of the national government's presence and capability is situated in the regional centre, and accessible more closely to its representative groups, should by itself go some way towards meeting this particular aspiration. But the aspiration could be met still further by the establishment of an elective regional consultative council or assembly. And here it is necessary to avoid being misled, by the common cant about 'talking shops' or by some of the more unsatisfactory features of the limited experience of regional economic planning councils, into assuming that any kind of regional consultative body lacking legislative or executive power of its own must necessarily be frustrated and useless. On the contrary, frustration is least likely to occur precisely in a situation of consultation only, where there is no expectation of exercising power which in the nature of things must in the end be subject to control and interference in the wider public interest by national government. Perhaps one of the main mistakes in the way the economic planning councils and boards were set up was to hold out the councils as having a special independent role, for which the boards were to advise and serve them. A much more productive approach would be to regard regional consultative councils or assemblies as being there to advise the regional level of national government – and, through it, the whole national government and Parliament.

Foreign countries' practice is not often very relevant to political possibilities in Britain, but it may be worth noting in this respect the experience in France. There it has been demonstrated that, in spite or perhaps even because of the retention of the complete integrity of the unitary power of the national government, it has been possible to develop a system of regional decentralisation in which a very substantial part of the national government's powers of planning and administration is exercised in each region by a co-ordinated team of resident national government staff, controlled by a resident very senior official representative of the head of state (the regional Prefect) who in turn is assisted by resident senior colleagues from the French Treasury and other ministries, and advised by a consultative body reflecting the region's interests – including elected representatives of local authorities.[22]

This kind of development, adapted to British circumstances and extended to its fullest practicable lengths in the ways suggested earlier, could be much more than a weak alternative to devolution of legislative or executive functions; it could be of positive and less dangerous benefit both to the regions themselves and to the effective government of the country as a whole. It could also facilitate, in a way that real devolution would not, a measure of useful further modernisation when the time is ripe in the boundaries and functions of local authorities and in their local/national relationship.

One final point must be made, reverting to a warning given earlier in this chapter. No kind of system for checking the centralising influence of national government can work very well anyway unless electors and politicians in the national Parliament both in and out of power are prepared to accept that, within reasonable limits, things can be done or allowed to happen in different ways and on a different scale (which means less as well as more) in different parts of the country, without there being any need to make a great song and dance about it at Westminster. There is very little evidence as yet that British politicians in practice are ever likely to accept this – or indeed that their constituents, even in Scotland or Wales, would applaud them if they did. In these circumstances, attempts on any significant scale to devolve legislative or executive power to new regional bodies could damage the national government capability but are unlikely to bring much in the way of compensating advantages. By contrast, many of those advantages could be achieved by leaving the national government power inviolate, decentralising its exercise, and developing institutions and practices to exploit that decentralisation.

NOTES AND REFERENCES

1 For example, Derek Senior in his chapter favours a species of water-divining. A more widespread preference is for a pattern based on the spheres of influence of the major conurbations, as evidenced

in matters such as employment, transport, and shopping and cultural facilities. But it has to be recognised that the boundaries likely in practice to be adopted in connection with any enhancement of the separate status of Scotland and Wales will be the historical ones which are already being used for purposes of administrative decentralisation; and in any further development of governmental regionalism within England itself one might do worse than follow the same course.

2 The appetite for regionalism grows by what it feeds on, even in national policy. Thus the habit of presenting unemployment figures regionally has tended to give a regional bias to the development both of political demand and of governmental thinking about economic policy – at the expense of possibilities requiring different-sized but less fashionable meshes of perception.

3 The unsuitability of the present local government pattern for purposes of planning in the fields of housing and industrial development, for example, is especially noticeable in the case of the metropolitan county boundaries, which tend to separate many of the problems from their most obvious solutions.

4 See *Memorandum of Dissent*, pp. 13–33, for an example of the persistence with which they reached this conclusion from the scanty available evidence.

5 The majority of the Kilbrandon Commission were quite clear that what might be expedient as regards Scotland and Wales was not necessarily appropriate to regions in England. Two of its members disagreed with this, but only on the ground that there should be an English voice heard in English affairs – see *Kilbrandon Report*, pp. 332–3; and this could in fact be achieved – if one wanted it – by providing a level of government for England as a whole, without going down to the level of its constituent regions.

6 Current discussions about devolution in Britain tend to skate round the lessons of Northern Ireland and its half-century of devolution within the UK, because of the special history and circumstances. But there are certain respects in which one cannot properly avoid taking warning from the experience of the Province. Part of the present trouble there (although admittedly only a part) arose because the Provincial government under a scheme of devolution had earlier been following policies and practices, presumably endorsed by the majority of its electorate, which the people and government of the United Kingdom as a whole were not prepared indefinitely to approve – or pay for; and when accordingly the UK government eventually sought with some success to induce a change of attitude in the Province, the necessary interference with the devolved powers aroused resentments which tended to aggravate the very situation that it was designed to relieve. Some English regions may one day have their majority/minority situations too, even though they are unlikely to be of such an acute kind.

7 See p. 160.

8 The evidence from occasional experiments in the past with overlord ministers, expected to exercise a general strategic function of this

kind in relation to departments that they did not themselves control, shows that even within the same level of government it is difficult to influence policy if you have not got specific power as well.

9 The analogy of a *ménage à trois* is a concession to the present-day tendency to think of everything in terms of sex. Older readers who remember their Gibbon may prefer to find their analogy in the theological controversies which once raged about the nature and internal relationships of the Trinity.

10 *Memorandum of Dissent*, para. 287(d).

11 Ibid., para. 295(a).

12 Ibid., para. 284.

13 See note 8 above.

14 *Memorandum of Dissent*, pp. 98–9.

15 Hence the noble enthusiasm of the patriotic declamations made in some of the ancient Greek city-states – and later in the Republic of Genoa.

16 Derek Senior's scheme for financing regional government out of the various kinds of taxation on motoring is an adaptation of a familiar old proposal for broadening the tax base of local authorities. Moving it from the local to the regional level does not make it much more credible.

17 *Kilbrandon Report*, para. 692.

18 Not that co-ordination, even when it *is* achieved, is relished by everyone. The late Mr R. H. S. Crossman has placed on record his dislike of the extent to which when he was Minister of Housing and Local Government his department collaborated with the departments of his Cabinet colleagues.

19 Connoisseurs of Civil Service-baiting will see the thread between Chapter 1 of the Fulton Report and the *Memorandum of Dissent.*

20 Not every government department at present has an office in every standard region. Such regional offices as do exist are of varying size and importance, and they are not fully co-ordinated with each other. The regional economic planning boards could be a means of modestly promoting more co-ordination, but one reason why they have not recently done or been encouraged to do much in this direction has been the uncertainty about the future created by the appointment of the Kilbrandon Commission and by the discussions following its Report.

21 Such a minister would be there to provide a political presence and not to pretend to any special power beyond what he derives from his own senior minister in Whitehall. But his presence as the political representative of the national government could nevertheless be useful not only for feedback but also for giving people in the region, including the government's own regional officials, a visible local point of political contact and communication.

22 A passing reference to regional government in France is made by Professor F. F. Ridley in his work for the Commission (Royal Commission on the Constitution, *The French Prefectoral System: an Example of Integrated Administrative Decentralisation*, Research

Paper 4, HMSO, 1973). Some may think that he understates the extent to which the French regional structure does in practice meet much of the kind of need which underlies many of the regionalist pressures in Britain. But of course it is difficult to disentangle the regional arrangements there from those for the *départements*.

Appendix: Summary of Schemes Recommended by the Royal Commission on the Constitution*

A. Legislative Devolution for Scotland and Wales

1. Legislative devolution was recommended for Scotland by eight of the thirteen members of the Commission and for Wales by six members.

General description

2. Responsibility for legislating on specifically defined matters would be transferred from the Westminster Parliament to directly elected Scottish and Welsh legislatures. In relation to the transferred subjects these legislatures would make such laws and policies as they saw fit, and would carry out all aspects of administration. The ultimate power and sovereignty of the United Kingdom Parliament would be preserved in all matters, but it would be a convention that in the ordinary course this power would not be used to legislate for Scotland or Wales on a transferred matter without the agreement of the Scottish or Welsh Government. The United Kingdom Government would also have the power, for use in exceptional circumstances, to determine, with the approval of the United Kingdom Parliament, that a Bill passed by the Scottish or Welsh legislature should not be submitted for the Royal Assent. The Scottish and Welsh executives would be composed of Ministers drawn from their respective assemblies who would then operate the traditional Cabinet system of government. It is the intention that the Scottish and Welsh Governments should have a large measure of financial

***This summary is reproduced directly from the consultative document *Devolution within the United Kingdom* (HMSO, 1974).**

independence, especially in matters of expenditure, but would be subject to such restraints as are necessary in the interests of the economic management of the United Kingdom as a whole.

Main features of the scheme

3. Legislative power in the following subjects would be transferred to the Scottish and Welsh legislative assemblies:

- Local government
- Town and country planning
- New towns
- Housing
- Building control
- Water supply and sewerage
- Ancient monuments and historic buildings
- Roads (including the construction, use and licensing of vehicles)
- Road passenger transport
- Harbours
- Other environmental services (*e.g.* prevention of pollution, coast protection and flood prevention)
- Education (probably excluding universities)
- Youth and community services
- Sports and recreation
- Arts and culture (including the Welsh and Gaelic languages)
- Social work services (including, for Scotland, probation and after-care)
- Health
- Miscellaneous regulatory functions (including matters such as betting, gaming, and lotteries, obscene publications, shop hours and liquor licensing)
- Agriculture, fisheries and food (except price support and some other functions)
- Forestry
- Crown estates
- Tourism

4. Legislative power in the following additional matters would be transferred to the Scottish Assembly only:

- Police
- Fire services
- Criminal policy and administration
- Prisons
- Administration of justice
- Legal matters, including law reform
- Highlands and Islands development (including crofting)
- Sea transport

5. In the subjects listed above the Westminster Parliament would normally cease to legislate for Scotland and Wales (though existing United Kingdom legislation in these fields would continue to apply initially). But the United Kingdom Parliament and Government would continue to be responsible for the international aspects of transferred matters. It is also envisaged that the Scottish and Welsh assemblies might have some limited powers in relation to consumer protection, road freight, civil aviation and broadcasting.

6. The legislative assemblies in Scotland and Wales would each have about 100 members directly elected for a fixed term of four years by the single transferable vote system of proportional representation, though in the more sparsely populated areas of Scotland the alternative vote system might be adopted. All matters relating to the franchise and to elections to the assembly (though not elections to local authorities) would be reserved to the United Kingdom Parliament.

7. The Scottish and Welsh executives would consist of Ministers drawn from their respective assemblies. Normally the leader of the majority party would be chief Minister (or Premier) and would form a Cabinet which would operate in accordance with the traditional Westminster principles of collective and ministerial responsibility. Scotland and Wales would each have a separate civil service.

8. Scotland and Wales would continue to be represented in the Westminster Parliament, but their representation in proportion to population would be the same as for England. This would probably reduce the number of Scottish MPs at Westminster from 71 to about 57; and the number of Welsh MPs from 36 to about 31.

9. The offices of Secretary of State for Scotland and Wales would disappear, but Scotland and Wales would each have a Minister with the special responsibility of representing its interests in the Cabinet.

10. There are detailed proposals for finance which the Report says are open to modification. The chief object would

be to give the Scottish and Welsh Governments maximum freedom in expenditure. Each would have its 'fair share of United Kingdom resources' and freedom to allocate expenditure on the transferred services according to its own chosen priorities. Scotland and Wales might also have some limited powers of independent taxation, and perhaps a share of United Kingdom taxes. But the assemblies' income would come mainly from United Kingdom subventions. They might also be able to raise loans to meet capital expenditure.

11. The determination of Scotland's and Wales' 'fair share of United Kingdom resources' would be in the hands of a nominated Exchequer Board which would be independent of the Scottish, Welsh and United Kingdom Governments. Exceptionally the United Kingdom Government could reject the Board's recommendation with the approval of the United Kingdom Parliament.

B. A Scheme for Elected Assemblies in Scotland, Wales and the English Regions

12. This scheme of intermediate level governments was the main proposal in the Memorandum of Dissent signed by two members of the Commission.

General description

13. The scheme seeks to achieve a substantial measure of devolution of power from the central Government to Scotland, Wales and the English regions. It could, however, be considered for application to Scotland and Wales alone. Under the scheme the United Kingdom Parliament and Government would remain responsible for the framework of legislation and major policy on all matters, but directly elected Scottish and Welsh and English regional assemblies would be responsible for adjusting United Kingdom policies to the special needs of their areas and putting them into effect. The Scottish, Welsh and English regional Governments would be run on the local authority pattern with a functional committee structure and not on the Cabinet model as in the scheme of legislative devolution. They would assume control of all the regional outposts of central Government now operating in their areas including the Scottish and Welsh Offices in their present form and the regional and local

offices of other central Government Departments. Thus these outposts, which employ very substantial numbers of civil servants, would be completely 'hived off' from central Government. The 'intermediate level' governments (*i.e.* the Scottish, Welsh and English regional governments) would also take over completely the functions of certain *ad hoc* authorities operating in their areas (*e.g.* health and water authorities); and they would be given some supervisory responsibilities in respect of the activities in their parts of the country of the various industrial and commercial authorities (*e.g.* gas and electricity boards). The 'intermediate level' governments would not be limited to the specific functions or duties conferred on them by Parliament; they would have a general residual competence to act for the welfare and good government of the people in their areas. They would have some independent revenue-raising powers and sufficient financial 'independence' of central Government to give them the requisite degree of freedom to carry out their duties and responsibilities.

Main features of the scheme

14. The scheme envisages that the broad range of functions set out in paragraph 13 above would be devolved to an assembly and government in Scotland, in Wales and in each of, say, five English regions. Each assembly would consist of about 100 members elected by the single transferable vote system of proportional representation for a fixed term of four years. The executive of each government would consist of a number of functional departments or divisions staffed by the authority's own civil servants. There would be departments or divisions for such functions as Finance, Education, Health and Social Security, the Environment, etc. Each department or division would be controlled by a committee drawn from the membership of the assembly – reflecting the balance of party strengths.

15. Each assembly would be able to make 'ordinances':

(*a*) to implement United Kingdom policies and legislation and to adapt them to the special needs of the area; and
(*b*) to give effect to their residual power to act for the welfare and good government of the people in the area.

16. Each intermediate level government would have its own civil service and a separate ombudsman There would be no change in the functions of local authorities, although they would deal with the appropriate intermediate government instead of with the central Government as at present. They would have direct representation in the intermediate level governments.

17. The general financial arrangements are outlined at the end of paragraph 13 above. A possible development of these arrangements is outlined in Appendix B of the Memorandum of Dissent. It is designed to give the intermediate level governments a considerable degree of financial and economic independence of central Government; and to improve the ability of the central Government to achieve the major objectives of national economic policy such as full employment, regionally and nationally, and a satisfactory rate of economic growth.

18. At the centre, the scheme envisages that Members of Parliament, by being relieved of a great deal of detail, would have time for a much greater share in Government policy making including more influence on the decisions which United Kingdom Ministers have to take in the Council of Ministers in Brussels; for these purposes MPs would need to be organised in functional committees matching each of the main Departments of Government. The composition of the House of Lords might be altered to include members of the 'intermediate level' governments.

19. The Secretaries of State for Scotland and Wales would remain as members of the United Kingdom Cabinet though their existing Departments would be taken over by the Scottish and Welsh Governments. They would have the special responsibility of safeguarding and promoting Scottish and Welsh interests in all Cabinet decisions. A third Cabinet Minister would perform a similar function for the English regions. There would be no reduction in the number of Scottish and Welsh MPs at Westminster.

C. Executive Devolution for Scotland, Wales and Eight English Regions

20. This scheme was recommended by two members who signed the Majority Report.

General description

21. The scheme seeks to achieve a substantial measure of devolution from the central Government to Scotland, Wales and the English regions. It is in essence a more restricted and less radical version of the scheme presented at B above. The United Kingdom Parliament and Government would be responsible for the framework of legislation and major policy in all matters, but wherever possible would transfer to directly elected assemblies in Scotland, Wales and eight English regions the responsibility, within that framework, for devising specific policies and executing them and for general administration. The intention would be to promote the maximum amount of regional participation and variation consistent with the general policy aims of the United Kingdom Government. The two members who support the scheme regard it as an essential feature that it should be applied in a more or less uniform way throughout Great Britain. It could, however, like Scheme B above, be considered for application to Scotland and Wales only.

22. Its main differences from Scheme B are:

(*a*) The assemblies would have no independent revenue raising powers.

(*b*) The assemblies would not have a residual competence to act for the welfare and good government of the people in their areas.

(*c*) The assemblies would not have the wide ordinance-making power proposed in Scheme B.

(*d*) The functions of the assemblies would be limited initially and increased in the light of experience; they would not necessarily take over *all* the existing executive functions of the Scottish Office and the Welsh Office, nor necessarily *all* the other outposts of central Government Departments operating in Scotland or Wales or in the English regions.

(*e*) The assemblies would not necessarily effect a general take-over of the work of the various non-industrial, non-commercial *ad hoc* authorities operating in their areas.

(*f*) The assemblies' relationship with local authorities in their areas might well be different from that envisaged in Scheme B (see paragraph 27 below).

(*g*) Scheme C does not recommend any changes in the institutions of central Government.

Main features of the scheme
23. Scotland, Wales and the eight English regions would each have an assembly of about 100 members directly elected by the single transferable vote system of proportional representation for a fixed term of four years. Each assembly would administer with as much freedom as possible the legislation and policies of the United Kingdom Parliament and Government.

24. Functions would be conferred on the assembly by the amendment of existing law and any new legislation relating to specific matters. Acts of Parliament would lay down policy in broad terms, authorising the assembly to fill in much of the detail – in some cases by statutory instruments. Executive authority would be vested not in Ministers but in the assembly itself, which would delegate much of its authority to functional committees, as local authorities now do. The transfer of functions would be a lengthy process, spread over many years. At first the assemblies would have a limited range of powers in matters such as strategic planning, but these powers would be gradually extended as time went on. Most of the existing executive functions of the Scottish and Welsh Offices would be devolved. Almost all subjects would offer some scope for regional involvement.

25. The regional assemblies would not have any independent revenue raising powers. They would be financed out of United Kingdom funds negotiated direct with the central Government. Their total expenditure would ultimately be for the United Kingdom Government to decide. The Government would also need to be satisfied that each assembly's proposed allocation of expenditure was broadly consistent with central policies. Subject to this the assembly would make its own expenditure decisions.

26. The scheme would not involve any change in Parliamentary representation, but it envisages that the separate offices of the Secretaries of State for Scotland and Wales would disappear. There would be a Minister with general responsibility for regional affairs.

27. The relationship between the regional assemblies and local government could develop in a number of different ways. Three possible ways are described:

- (*a*) local authorities could be completely subordinate to the regional government and it would be for each regional government to decide on the distribution of functions between itself and its local authorities;
- (*b*) local and regional authorities could each be autonomous in functions allocated to them from the centre, and could work in parallel; local authorities would remain accountable for the proper performance of their functions to the United Kingdom Government;
- (*c*) the relationship between local and regional government could depend on what Parliament considered appropriate in each separate field of legislation.

28. The precise relationship between the regional assemblies and *ad hoc* bodies would depend on a detailed review.

D. Welsh Advisory Council

29. Three members who signed the Majority Report recommend the establishment of a Welsh Advisory Council.

General description

30. The reasoning behind this scheme is that Wales has derived great benefit from the comparatively recent appointment of its Secretary of State, and that the economic and other problems facing the Principality can best be dealt with through the development and retention of that office. So the scheme aims to reconcile the continued existence of the Secretary of State and the Welsh Office in its present form with the widely expressed desire for a directly elected assembly to act as the voice of Wales. Accordingly there would be a directly elected Welsh Council to advise the Secretary of State and to scrutinise the operation of Government policies and agencies in Wales.

Main features of the scheme

31. The Welsh Advisory Council would be directly elected by the single transferable vote system of proportional representation and would consist of about 60 members. It would replace the existing nominated Welsh Council. It

would have no legislative, executive or administrative powers. Its functions would be to scrutinise, debate and make representations to the Secretary of State about Government policies and activities in Wales, including the activities of the nationalised industries and other *ad hoc* bodies operating there. It would inevitably be interested in, but would in no sense supervise, the activities of local authorities.

32. The Council's scrutiny would range over such matters as the Welsh economy, employment, major road development and land use proposals, public services and the Welsh language. It would also hold an annual debate on the Government's expenditure proposals for Wales. It would operate through standing committees and be financed from the United Kingdom Exchequer. It would also have the right to nominate some members of *ad hoc* bodies operating in Wales.

33. The Secretary of State and other Welsh Ministers would on invitation attend the Council to explain policy, answer criticisms and receive advice. Officials of the Welsh Office would also be invited to report to the Council and to answer questions on their activities. Members of Parliament from Welsh constituencies might attend and speak, but not vote, at the Council's plenary sessions.

E. A Scottish Council with Advisory and Legislative Functions

34. One member who signed the Majority Report recommended the establishment of a Scottish Council with advisory and legislative functions.

General description

35. There would be a directly elected Scottish Council which would have the same advisory functions as proposed for the Welsh Council and summarised at paragraphs 30 to 33 above. In addition, however, the Scottish Council would have some powers in relation to Scottish legislation. Thus it would take the Second Reading, Committee and Report stages of Scottish Bills referred to it by the House of Commons. Unless a Bill was then recalled by the Leader of the House, the Scottish Council would be able to give it a Third Reading and

submit it for Royal Assent without any reference back to the House of Commons and without any passage through the House of Lords.

F. Regional Co-ordinating and Advisory Councils for the English Regions

36. Eight members of the Commission recommended this scheme for English regional councils with advisory and co-ordinating powers.

General description

37. The scheme is based on the view that it would not be right for the English regions to be given any legislative or executive powers now exercised by central Government, and that it would be illogical (following the recent reorganisation of local authorities) for them to take over powers from local government. Yet at the regional level it is believed that there is scope for more effective co-operation between local authorities and a need for more open discussion and democratic influence on those matters affecting the region which are decided by central Government or by *ad hoc* bodies. To meet this need, and to give advice to the central Government on regional problems, there would be regional councils primarily composed of local government councillors.

Main features of the scheme

38. There would be eight English regions (*i.e.* those that have already been established for economic planning purposes). Each region would have an advisory council which would consist of about 60 members. Four-fifths of the members of each council would be members of the local authorities in the region and would be 'elected' by those local authorities to membership of the regional advisory council. One-fifth of the members would be nominated by the central Government to secure representation from industry and commerce, trade unions, education and other interests.

39. The regional advisory councils would have no legislative, executive or administrative powers. Their functions would be to:–

(*a*) take over the functions of the present nominated regional economic planning councils;

(*b*) advise on Government spending in their regions;

(*c*) advise and make representations to central Government about Government policies and activities generally in their regions, including the operations of nationalised industries and other *ad hoc* bodies (some of whose members they would nominate);

(*d*) have a mainly co-ordinating function in the field of local government.

40. Under (*d*) it is envisaged that the regional council would play an important part in the formulation of the broad economic and land use strategy which would be the regional framework within which central and local government services would be provided. The structure plans of local authorities would have to fit into this general strategy and would be submitted for Ministerial approval through the regional council with its comments. The council would by agreement promote and co-ordinate action by local government in the region. It would have no power of direction over local authorities in the region and would not itself administer services or undertake works.

41. In carrying out their functions the councils would ordinarily meet in public. They would elect their own chairmen.

G. A Scheme for Co-ordinating Committees of Local Authorities

42. This scheme is recommended for England by one member of the Commission.

General description

43. The scheme is based on the view that in England the best way of devolving power from the centre is to concentrate on strengthening the power of the new larger local authorities. It is envisaged that if this were done the only need at regional level would be to co-ordinate the planning activities of local authorities. Instead of the present voluntary co-operation between local authorities there would be established a formal system of regional committees. Each would consist entirely of indirectly elected representatives of local authorities and there would be no provision for nominated members. It would be mandatory for local authorities to submit their

plans for the regional committee and obtain its comments before submitting them for Ministerial approval. The present economic planning councils would be abolished. It is envisaged that the scheme might be combined with regional committees of the House of Commons which might vet regional plans and Government expenditure in the regions.